Rick Steves'®

SNAPSHOT

Northern Ireland

Rick Steves & Pat O'Connor

CONTENTS

INTRODUCTION

This Snapshot guide, excerpted from my guidebook *Rick Steves' Ireland 2010,* introduces you to Northern Ireland—an underrated and often overlooked part of the Emerald Isle that surprises visitors with its friendliness. I've included a lively mix of cities (Belfast and Derry), smaller towns (Portrush and Bangor), and plenty of lazy countryside sights. History is palpable atop the brooding walls of Derry and in the remote and traditional County Donegal (actually just over the border, in the Republic of Ireland). And, while it's perfectly safe for a visit, Northern Ireland gives you a feel for Ireland's 20th-century "Troubles" as nowhere else—especially the provocative political murals in Derry's Bogside neighborhood, and on Belfast's Falls Road and Shankill Road. But you'll also find enjoyable escapes: From the breezy seaside resort of Portrush, you can visit the scenic Antrim Coast—which boasts the unique staggered-columns geology of the Giant's Causeway, the spectacularly set Dunluce Castle, and a chance to sample whiskey at Old Bushmills Distillery.

To help you have the best trip possible, I've included the following topics in this book:

• **Planning Your Time,** with advice on how to make the most of your limited time

• **Orientation,** including tourist information (abbreviated as TI), tips on public transportation, local tour options, and helpful hints

• **Sights** with ratings:

▲▲▲—Don't miss

▲▲—Try hard to see

▲—Worthwhile if you can make it

No rating—Worth knowing about

• **Sleeping** and **Eating,** with good-value recommendations in every price range

• **Connections,** with tips on trains, buses, and driving

Practicalities, near the end of this book, has information on money, phoning, hotel reservations, transportation, and more.

To travel smartly, read this little book in its entirety before you go. It's my hope that this guide will make your trip more meaningful and rewarding. Traveling like a temporary local, you'll get the absolute most out of every mile, minute, and pound.

Happy travels!

Rick Steves

NORTHERN IRELAND

NORTHERN IRELAND

The island of Ireland was once a colony of Great Britain. Unlike its Celtic cousins, Scotland and Wales, Ireland has always been distant from London—due more to its Catholicism than the Irish Sea.

Four hundred years ago, Protestant settlers from England and Scotland were strategically "planted" in Catholic Ireland to help assimilate the island into the British economy. These settlers established their own cultural toehold on the island, while the Catholic Irish held strong to their Gaelic culture.

Over the centuries, British rule has not been easy. By the beginning of the 20th century, the sparse Protestant population could no longer control the entire island. When Ireland won its independence in 1921 (after a bloody guerrilla war against British rule), 26 of the island's 32 counties became the Irish Free State, ruled from Dublin with dominion status in the British Commonwealth—similar to Canada. In 1949, they left the Commonwealth and became the Republic of Ireland, severing all political ties with Britain.

Meanwhile, the six remaining northeastern counties (the only ones with a Protestant majority) chose not to join the Irish Free State in 1922, and remained part of the UK.

In this new political entity called Northern Ireland, the long-established Orange Order and the military muscle of the newly mobilized Ulster Volunteer Force (UVF) worked to defend the union with Britain—so their political philosophy was "Unionist." This was countered on the Catholic side by the Irish Republican Army (IRA), which wanted all 32 of Ireland's counties to be united in one Irish nation—their political goals were "Nationalist."

In World War II, the Republic stayed neutral while the North enthusiastically supported the Allied cause—winning a spot close to London's heart. Londonderry (Derry) became an essential Allied convoy port, while Belfast lost more than 800 civilians during two Luftwaffe bombing raids. After the war, the split between North and South seemed permanent, and Britain invested heavily in Northern Ireland to bring it solidly into the UK fold.

With 94 percent of the Republic of Ireland (the South) Catholic and only 6 percent Protestant, there was no question as to which group was dominant. But at the time the North was formed, the Catholics, although a minority, were still a sizable 35 percent and demanded attention. Discrimination was considered necessary to maintain the Protestant status quo in the North, leading to the Troubles that filled headlines from the late 1960s to the mid-1990s.

This has never been a fight over Protestant and Catholic religious differences—it's about whether Northern Ireland will stay part of the UK or become part of the Republic of Ireland. The indigenous Irish of Northern Ireland, who generally want to unite with Ireland, happen to be Catholic. The descendants of the Scottish and English settlers, who generally want to remain part of Britain, happen to be Protestant.

Partly inspired by Martin Luther King Jr. and the civil rights movement in America in the 1960s—beamed into Irish living rooms by the new magic of television news—the Catholic minority in Northern Ireland began a nonviolent struggle to end discrimination, advocating for better jobs and housing. Extremists polarized issues, and demonstrations—also caught on TV news—became violent.

Northern Ireland Almanac

Official Name: Since Northern Ireland is not an independent state, there is no official country name. Some call it Ulster, while others label it the Six Counties. Politically, it's the smallest province of the UK (the other three provinces are England, Wales, and Scotland).

Population: Northern Ireland's 1.7 million people are about 40 percent Protestant (mostly Presbyterian and Anglican) and 40 percent Catholic. Another 5 percent profess different religions, and 15 percent claim no religious ties. English is far and away the chief language, though Gaelic (Irish) is also spoken.

Despite the country's genetic homogeneity, the population is highly segregated along political, religious, and cultural lines. Roughly speaking, the eastern seaboard is more Unionist, Protestant, and of English-Scottish heritage, while the south and west (bordering the Republic of Ireland) are Nationalist, Catholic, and of Irish descent. Cities are often clearly divided between neighborhoods of one group or the other. Early in life, locals learn to identify the highly symbolic (and highly charged) colors, jewelry, music, and vocabulary that distinguish the cultural groups.

Latitude and Longitude: 54°N and 5°W. It's a similar latitude to the Alaskan panhandle.

Area: 5,400 square miles (about the size of Connecticut), constituting a sixth of the island. Northern Ireland includes 6 of the island's traditional 32 counties.

Geography: Northern Ireland is shaped roughly like a doughnut, with the UK's largest lake in the middle (Lough Neagh, 150 square miles and a prime eel fishery). The terrain comprises gently rolling hills of green grass, rising to 2,800-foot Slieve Donard. The weather is temperate, cloudy, moist, windy, and hard to predict.

Biggest Cities: Belfast, the capital, has 300,000 residents. Half a million people—nearly one in three Northern Irish—inhabit the greater Belfast area. Derry (called Londonderry by Unionists) has 84,000 people.

Economy: Northern Ireland's economy is more closely tied to the UK than to the Republic of Ireland. Sectarian violence has held back growth, and the economy gets subsidies from the UK and the EU. Traditional agriculture (potatoes and grain) is fad-

Unionists were afraid that if the island became one nation, the relatively poor Republic of Ireland would drag down the comparatively affluent North, and the high percentage of Catholics could mean repression of the Protestants. As Protestants and Catholics clashed in 1969, the British Army entered the fray. Their peacekeeping role gradually evolved into acting as muscle for the Unionist government. In 1972, a watershed year, more than 500 died as combatants

ing fast, though modern techniques and abundant grassland make Northern Ireland a major producer of sheep, cows, and grass seed. Modern software and communications companies are replacing old traditional manufacturing. Shipyards are rusty relics, and the linen industry is now threadbare; both are victims of cheaper labor available in Asia.

Currency: Northern Ireland uses not the euro, but the pound (£). Exchange rate: £1 = about $1.60.

Government: Northern Ireland is not a self-governing nation, but is part of the UK, ruled from London by Queen Elizabeth II and Prime Minister Gordon Brown, and represented in Parliament by 18 elected Members of Parliament. For 50 years (1922–1972), Northern Ireland was granted a great deal of autonomy and self-governance, known as "Home Rule." The current National Assembly (108-seat Parliament)—after an ineffective five years due to political logjams—recently began to show signs of rejuvenation.

Politics are dominated, of course, by the ongoing debate between Unionists (who want to preserve the union with the UK) and Nationalists (who want to join the Republic of Ireland). Two high-profile and controversial figures have been at the opposite ends of this debate: the elderly firebrand Reverend Ian Paisley for the Unionists (who retired in 2008); and assassination-attack survivor Gerry Adams of Sinn Fein, the political arm of the IRA. In a hopeful development in the spring of 2007, the two allowed themselves to be photographed together across a negotiation table (a moment both had once sworn would never happen) as London returned control of the government to Belfast.

Flag: The official flag of Northern Ireland is the Union flag of the UK. But you'll also see the green, white, and orange Irish tricolor (waved by Nationalists) and the Northern Irish flag (white with a red cross and a red hand at its center), which is used by Unionists.

moved from petrol bombs to guns, and a new, more violent IRA emerged. In that chapter of the struggle for an independent and united Ireland, more than 3,000 people were killed.

A 1985 agreement granted Dublin a consulting role in the Northern Ireland government. Unionists bucked this idea, and violence escalated. That same year, Belfast City Hall draped a huge, defiant banner under its dome, proclaiming, *Belfast Says No.*

In 1994, the banner came down. In the 1990s—with Ireland's membership in the EU, the growth of its economy, and the weakening of the Catholic Church's influence—the consequences of a united Ireland became slightly less threatening to the Unionists. Also in 1994, the IRA declared a cease-fire, and the Protestant Ulster Volunteer Force (UVF) followed suit.

The Nationalists wanted British troops out of Northern Ireland, while the Unionists demanded that the IRA turn in its arms. Optimists hailed the signing of a breakthrough peace plan in 1998, called the "Good Friday Accord" by Nationalists, or the "Belfast Agreement" by Unionists. This led to the emotional release of prisoners on both sides in 2000.

Recently, additional progress has taken place on both fronts. The IRA finally "verifiably put their arms beyond use" in 2005, and backed the political process. In 2009, most Loyalist paramilitary groups did the same. Meanwhile, British Army surveillance towers were dismantled in 2006, and the army formally ended its 38-year-long Operation Banner campaign in 2007. Major hurdles to a lasting peace persist, but the downtown checkpoints are history, and the "bomb-damage clearance sales" are over. And today, more tourists than ever are venturing north to Belfast and Derry.

Terminology

Ulster (one of Ireland's four ancient provinces) consists of nine counties in the northern part of the island of Ireland. Six of these make up Northern Ireland (pronounced "Norn Iron" by locals), while three counties remain part of the Republic.

Unionists—and the more hard-line, working-class **Loyalists**—want the North to remain in the UK. The **Ulster Unionist Party (UUP),** the political party representing moderate Unionist views, is currently led by Sir Reg Empey (after being headed for years by Nobel Peace Prize co-winner David Trimble). The **Democratic Unionist Party (DUP),** led by Peter Robinson (protégé of the recently retired Reverend Ian Paisley), takes a harder stance in defense of Unionism. The **Ulster Volunteer Force (UVF),** the **Ulster Freedom Fighters (UFF),** and the **Ulster Defense Association (UDA)** are the Loyalist paramilitary organizations mentioned most frequently in newspapers and on spray-painted walls.

Nationalists—and the more hard-line, working-class **Republicans**—want a united and independent Ireland ruled by Dublin. The **Social Democratic Labor Party (SDLP),** founded by Nobel Peace Prize co-winner John Hume and currently led by Mark Durkan, is the moderate political party representing Nationalist views. **Sinn Fein** (shin fayn), led by Gerry Adams, takes a harder stance in defense of Nationalism. The **Irish Republican Army**

(IRA) is the Nationalist paramilitary organization (linked with Sinn Fein) mentioned most often in the press and in graffiti.

To gain more insight into the complexity of the Troubles, see the University of Ulster's informative and evenhanded Conflict Archive at http://cain.ulst.ac.uk/index.html.

Safety

Tourists in Northern Ireland are no longer considered courageous (or reckless). When a local spots you with a lost look on your face, they're likely to ask, "Wot yer lookin fer?" in their distinctive Northern accent. They're not suspicious of you, but rather trying to help you find your way. You're safer in Belfast than in any other UK city—and far safer than in most major US cities. You have to look for trouble to find it here. Just don't seek out spit-and-sawdust pubs in working-class Protestant neighborhoods and sing Catholic songs.

Tourists notice the tension mainly during the "marching season" (Easter–Aug, peaking in early July). July 12—"the Twelfth"—is traditionally the most confrontational day of the year in the North, when proud Protestant Unionist Orangemen march to celebrate their Britishness and their separate identity from the Republic of Ireland (often through staunchly Nationalist Catholic neighborhoods). Lay low if you stumble onto any big Orange parades.

Northern Ireland Is a Different Country

The border is almost invisible. But when you leave the Republic of Ireland and enter Northern Ireland, you *are* crossing an international border. Although you don't have to flash your passport, you do change stamps, phone cards, money—and your Eurailpass is no longer valid. Gas is more expensive in Northern Ireland than in the Republic (so fill up before crossing the border). However, groceries are 25 percent cheaper. These price differences create a lively, daily shopping trade for those living near the border.

You won't use euros here; Northern Ireland issues its own Ulster pound, which, like the Scottish pound, is interchangeable with the English pound (€1 = about £0.85; £1 = about $1.60). Some establishments near the border may take your euros, but at a lousy exchange rate. So keep any euros for your return to the Republic, and get pounds from an ATM inside Northern Ireland instead. And if you're heading to England next, it's best to change your Ulster pounds into English ones (free at any bank in Northern Ireland, England, Wales, or Scotland).

BELFAST

Seventeenth-century Belfast was just a village. With the influx, or "plantation," of English and (more often) Scottish settlers, the character of the place changed. After the Scots and English were brought in—and the native Irish were subjugated—Belfast boomed, spurred by the success of the local linen, rope-making, and shipbuilding industries. The Industrial Revolution took root with a vengeance. While the rest of Ireland remained rural and agricultural, Belfast earned its nickname ("Old Smoke") during the time when many of the brick buildings that you'll see today were built. The year 1888 marked the birth of modern Belfast. After Queen Victoria granted city status to this boomtown of 300,000, its citizens built the city's centerpiece, City Hall.

Belfast is the birthplace of the *Titanic* (and many other ships that didn't sink). Two huge, mustard-colored cranes (once the biggest in the world, nicknamed Samson and Goliath) rise like skyscrapers above the harbor. They stand idle now, but serve as a reminder of this town's former shipbuilding might.

Today, investments from south of the border—the Republic of Ireland—are injecting quiet optimism into the dejected shipyards where the *Titanic* was built, developing the historic Titanic Quarter. Cranes are building condos along the rejuvenated Lagan riverfront.

It feels like a new morning in Belfast. It's hard to believe that the bright and bustling pedestrian center was once a subdued, traffic-free security zone. Now there's no hint of security checks, once a tiresome daily routine. These days, both Catholics and Protestants are rooting for the Belfast Giants ice hockey team, one of many reasons to live together peacefully.

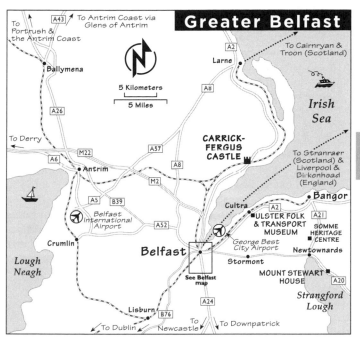

Still, it's a fragile peace and a tenuous hope. Mean-spirited murals, hateful bonfires built a month before they're actually burned, and pubs with security gates are reminders that the island is split—and 800,000 Protestant Unionists in the North prefer it that way.

Planning Your Time

Big Belfast is thin on sights. For most, one day of sightseeing is plenty.

Day Trip from Dublin: On the handy, two-hour Dublin–Belfast train (cheap, €38 "day-return" tickets, €52 round-trip with return on a different day; can cost more Fri–Sun, often substantial discounts for booking online), you could make Belfast a day trip: 7:35–Catch the early-morning train from Dublin and arrive in Belfast at 9:50; 11:00–City Hall tour (Mon–Fri), browse the pedestrian zone, lunch, ride a shared black taxi up Falls Road; 15:00-side-trip to the Ulster Folk and Transport Museum; evening–Return to Dublin (last train Mon–Sat departs Belfast at 20:10 and arrives in Dublin at 22:20). Sunday's trains depart later and return earlier, compressing your already limited time in Belfast (first train departs Dublin at 10:00 and arrives in Belfast at 12:15; last train departs Belfast at 19:00 and pulls into Dublin at 21:05). Confirm train times at local stations. Note that the TI offers the Historic

Belfast Walk at 14:00 on Wednesday, Friday, and Saturday, as well as summer Sundays (June–Sept). On Friday and Saturday, St. George's Market bustles in the morning. On Saturday, the only tour of City Hall is at 14:00 and 15:00 (Oct–May only at 14:30, no tours on Sun year-round).

Staying Overnight: Belfast makes a pleasant overnight stop, with plenty of cheap hostels, reasonable B&Bs, weekend hotel deals (Fri–Sun), and a resort neighborhood full of B&Bs 30 minutes away in Bangor.

Two Days in Belfast: Choose among the Living History bus tour, Ulster Folk and Transport Museum (in nearby Cultra), Botanic Gardens, and Carrickfergus Castle. Or take a day trip to the Antrim Coast.

Two Days in Small-Town Northern Ireland: From Dublin (via Belfast), take the train to Portrush; allow two nights and a day to tour the Causeway Coast (castle, whiskey distilleries, Giant's Causeway, resort fun), then follow the Belfast-in-a-day plan described earlier. With a third day, add Derry.

Coming from Scotland: With good ferry connections (from Stranraer or Troon in Scotland, or Liverpool in England; see "Belfast Connections"), it's easy to begin your exploration of the Emerald Isle in Belfast, then head south to Dublin and the Republic.

Orientation to Belfast

(area code: 028)

For the first-time visitor in town for a quick look, Belfast is pretty simple. Locate these four useful landmarks on your map, and use

them to navigate as you stroll the town (listed from north to south): Albert Clock Tower, City Hall, Shaftesbury Square, and Queens University.

There are three zones of interest: **central** (Donegall Square, City Hall, pedestrian shopping, TI), **southern** (Botanic Gardens, university, Ulster Museum), and **western** (working-class sectarian neighborhoods west of the freeway). Belfast's "Golden Mile"—stretching from Hotel Europa to the university district—connects the central and southern zones with many of the best dinner and entertainment spots.

Tourist Information
For Belfast
The modern TI (look for *Welcome Centre* signs) has fine, free city maps and an enjoyable bookshop with Internet access (June–Sept Mon–Sat 9:00–19:00, Sun 11:00–16:00; Oct–May Mon–Sat 9:00–17:30, Sun 11:00–16:00; one block north of City Hall at 47 Donegall Place, tel. 028/9024-6609, www.gotobelfast.com). City walking tours depart from the TI (see "Tours in Belfast"). For the latest on evening fun, get *The List* free at the TI or *That's Entertainment* at newsstands (50p).

For the Republic of Ireland
Traveling on to the Republic of Ireland, are ye? If it's information you'll be wanting, 'tis the place for you to go (Mon–Fri 9:00–17:00, closed Sat–Sun, 53 Castle Street, off Donegall Place, tel. 028/9026-5500, www.discoverireland.ie).

Arrival in Belfast
Arriving by fast train, you'll go directly to Central Station (with ATMs and free city maps at ticket counter). From the station, a free Centerlink bus loops to Donegall Square, with stops near Shaftesbury Square (recommended hostels), the bus station (some recommended hotels), and the TI (free with any train or bus ticket, 4/hr, never on Sun; during morning rush hour, bus runs only between station and Donegall Square). Allow about £4 for a taxi from Central Station to Donegall Square, or £6 to my B&B listings in south Belfast.

Slower trains arc through Belfast, stopping at several downtown stations, including Central Station, Great Victoria Station (most central, near Donegall Square and most hotels), Botanic Station (close to the university, Botanic Gardens, and some recommended hostels), and Adelaide (near several recommended B&Bs). It's easy and cheap to connect stations by train (£1).

Helpful Hints
US Consulate: It's at Danesfort House (Mon–Fri 8:30–17:00, closed Sat–Sun, 233 Stranmillis Road, www.usembassy.org .uk).

Market: On Friday and Saturday mornings (roughly until 14:00), **St. George's Market** is a commotion of clothes, produce, and seafood (at corner of Oxford and East Bridge Streets, five blocks east of Donegall Square, tel. 028/9043-5704).

Shopping Mall: Victoria Square is a glitzy American-style mall. Its huge glass dome reflects Belfast's economic rejuvenation (Mon–Tue 9:00–19:00, Wed–Fri 9:00–21:00, Sat 9:00–18:00,

Sun 13:00–18:00; 3 blocks east of City Hall—bordered by Chichester, Victoria, Ann, and Montgomery streets; www .victoriasquare.com).

Phone Tips: To call the Republic of Ireland from Northern Ireland, dial 00-353, then the area code without its initial 0, then the local number. To call Northern Ireland from the Republic of Ireland, dial 048, then the local eight-digit number.

Internet Access: Located near the Belfast International City Hostel, **Revelations Internet Café** is at 27 Shaftesbury Square (£4/hr, Mon–Fri 8:00–22:00, Sat 10:00–18:00, Sun 11:00–19:00, tel. 028/9032-0337).

Post Office: The main post office, with lots of fun postcards, is at the intersection of High and Bridge Streets (Mon–Fri 9:00–17:30, Sat 9:00-12:30, closed Sun, 3 long blocks north of Donegall Square).

Laundry: Globe Launderers is at 37–39 Botanic Avenue (£5 self-serve, £7.50 drop-off service, Mon–Fri 8:00–21:00, Sat 8:00–18:00, Sun 12:00–18:00, tel. 028/9024-3956). For the B&B neighborhood south of town, the closest is **Whistle Laundry** (£7.50 drop-off service, Mon–Fri 8:30–18:00, Sat 8:30–17:30, closed Sun, 160 Lisburn Road, at intersection with Eglantine Avenue, tel. 028/9038-1297).

Bike Rental: McConvey Cycles is at 183 Ormeau Road (£15/24 hrs, Mon–Sat 9:00–18:00, Thu until 20:00, closed Sun, tel. 028/9033-0322, www.rentabikebelfast.com).

Queens University Student Union: Located directly across University Road from the red-brick University building, the Student Union is just as handy for tourists as it is for college students. Inside you'll find an ATM (at end of main hall, on the right), WCs, a pharmacy, a mini-market, and Wi-Fi. Grab a quick and cheap £4 sandwich and coffee at **Clement's Coffee Shop** (Mon–Fri 8:30–22:30, Sat 9:00–22:00, closed Sun).

Getting Around Belfast

If you line up your sightseeing logically, you can do most of the town on foot.

Ask about "Day Tracker" tickets that give individuals one day of unlimited train and bus travel anywhere in Northern Ireland for £15 (making it easy to side-trip to Bangor, the Ulster Folk and Transport Museum in Cultra, or Carrickfergus Castle). Families (up to two adults and two kids under 16) visiting in July and August get an even better deal: the £18 one-day Family Pass, valid for train and bus travel. Buy your pass at any train station in the city. A "day return" ticket to Carrickfergus Castle, Cultra, or Bangor is always cheaper than buying two one-way tickets.

For information on trains and buses in Belfast, contact Translink (tel. 028/9066-6630, www.translink.co.uk).

By Bus: Buses go from Donegall Square East to Malone Road and my recommended B&Bs (#8B or #8C, 3/hr, £1.50, all-day pass costs £3.50 before 10:00 and £2.70 after).

By Taxi: Taxis are reasonable and should be considered. Rather than use their meters, many cabs charge a flat £4 rate for any ride up to two miles. It's £1.50 per mile after that. Ride a shared cab if you're going up Falls Road (explained later in "Sights in Belfast").

Tours in Belfast

▲**Walking Tours**—The **Historic Belfast Walk** takes you through the historic core of town (£6, 90 min; departs from TI at 14:00 on Wed, Fri, and Sat—June–Sept also on Sun; confirm tour times with TI, book in advance, tel. 028/9024-6609).

Mixing drinks and history, **Historical Pub Tours of Belfast** offers two-hour walking tours that start at the Crown Dining Room pub and end six pubs later (£6; May–Oct Thu at 19:00, Sat at 16:00; book in advance, meet at pub above Crown Liquor Saloon at 46 Great Victoria Street across from Hotel Europa, tel. 028/9268-3665, www.belfastpubtours.com).

Coiste Irish Political Tours leads extended, three-hour walks along the Falls Road to explain the history of the neighborhood from an intensely Republican perspective. Led by former IRA prisoners, you'll visit murals, gardens of remembrance, peace walls, and community centers in this rejuvenating section of gritty Belfast. Tours meet beside the Divis Tower (the 20-story apartment house at the east end of the Divis Road near the A-12 Westlink motorway overpass) and end at the Milltown Cemetery (£8, daily at 11:00, tel. 028/9020-0770, www.coiste.ie, Seamus Kelley).

▲**Big Bus Tours**—**City Sightseeing**'s Living History Tour is the best introduction to the city's recent and complicated political and social history. You'll cruise the Catholic and Protestant working-class neighborhoods, with a commentary explaining the political murals and places of interest—mostly dealing with the Troubles of the last 40 years. You see things from the bus and get out only for photos (£12.50, 90 min, daily on the hour 10:00–16:30, fewer tours in winter—call first; depart from corner of Royal Avenue and Castle Place across from McDonald's, 2 blocks north of Donegall Square; pay cash at kiosk or on bus, or book by phone with credit card, tel. 028/9045-9035, www.city-sightseeing.com).

BELFAST

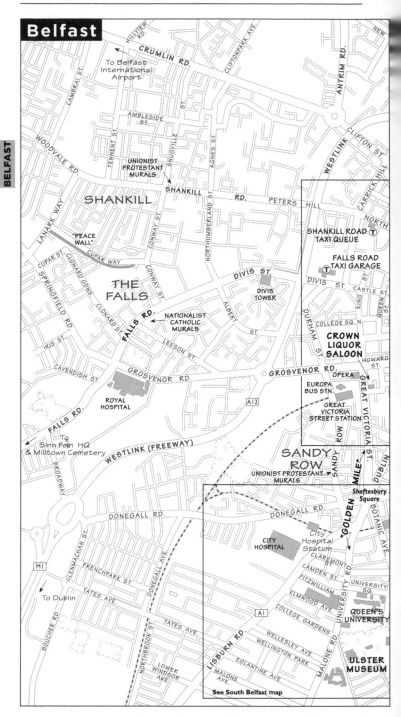

Belfast

CRUMLIN RD.

To Belfast
International
Airport

HILLVIEW RD.

CLIFTONPARK AVE.

CAMBRAI ST.

AMBLESIDE ST.

TENENT ST.

SNUGVILLE ST.

AGNES ST.

ANTRIM RD.

NEW

WOODVALE RD.

UNIONIST
PROTESTANT
MURALS

SHANKILL

SHANKILL   RD.

PETERS HILL

CLIFTON ST.

WESTLINK

CARRICK HILL

NORTH

LANARK WAY

"PEACE
WALL"

CUPAR WAY

CONWAY ST.

NORTHUMBERLAND ST.

SHANKILL ROAD
TAXI QUEUE (T)

FALLS ROAD (T)
TAXI GARAGE

CUPAR ST.

CLONARD GDNS.

SPRINGFIELD RD.

CLONARD ST.

THE
FALLS

CONWAY ST.

DIVIS ST.

DIVIS
TOWER

DIVIS ST.

CASTLE ST.

KING ST.

QUEEN ST.

IRIS ST.

NATIONALIST
CATHOLIC
MURALS

ALBERT ST.

FALLS RD.

LEESON ST.

COLLEGE SQ. N.

DURHAM ST.

CROWN
LIQUOR
SALOON

HOWARD
ST.

CAVENDISH ST.

GROSVENOR RD.

GROSVENOR RD.

EUROPA BUS STN.

OPERA

GREAT VICTORIA ST.

ROYAL
HOSPITAL

A12

GREAT
VICTORIA
STREET STATION

FALLS RD.

To
Sinn Fein HQ
& Milltown Cemetery

WESTLINK (FREEWAY)

SANDY
ROW

UNIONIST PROTESTANT
MURALS

SANDY ROW

"GOLDEN MILE"

DUBLIN RD.

BROADWAY

Shaftesbury
Square

BOTANIC AVE.

DONEGALL RD.

DONEGALL RD.

City
Hospital
Station

CLAREMONT

M1

GLENMACHAN ST.

FRENCHPARK ST.

CITY
HOSPITAL

CAMDEN ST.

UNIVERSITY RD.

UNIVERSITY
SQ.

To Dublin

TATES AVE.

DONEGALL AVE.

FITZWILLIAM

ELMWOOD AVE.

BOUCHER RD.

A1

COLLEGE GARDENS

QUEEN'S
UNIVERSITY

NORTHBROOK ST.

TATES AVE.

LISBURN RD.

WELLESLEY AVE.

WELLINGTON PARK

MALONE RD.

ULSTER
MUSEUM

LOWER
WINDSOR
AVE.

EGLANTINE AVE.

MALONE
AVE.

See South Belfast map

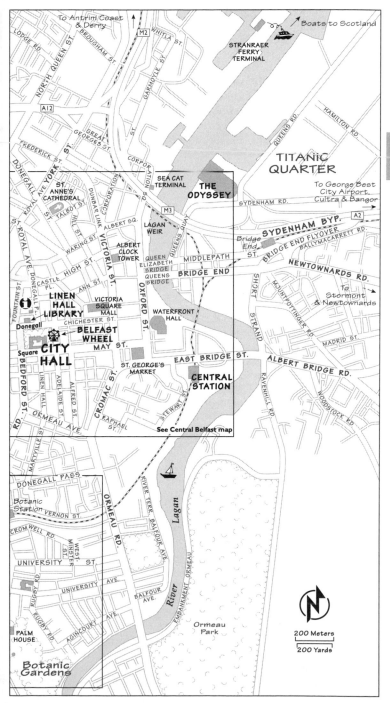

BELFAST

To Antrim Coast & Derry

Boats to Scotland

STRANRAER FERRY TERMINAL

M2

WHITLA ST.

GARMOYLE ST.

BROUGHAM ST.

NORTH QUEEN ST.

LODGE RD.

A12

GREAT GEORGES ST.

FREDERICK ST.

CORPORATION

ST.

QUEENS RD.

HAMILTON RD.

TITANIC QUARTER

SEA CAT TERMINAL

THE ODYSSEY

To George Best City Airport, Cultra & Bangor

SYDENHAM RD.

M3

SYDENHAM BYP.

A2

DONEGALL ST.

ROYAL AVE.

YORK ST.

ST. ANNE'S CATHEDRAL

TALBOT ST.

DUNBAR LINK

ALBERT SQ.

VICTORIA ST.

WARING ST.

HILL ST.

ALBERT CLOCK TOWER

Lagan Weir

QUEENS QUAY

MIDDLEPATH

Bridge End

BRIDGE END FLYOVER

BALLYMACARRETT RD.

NEWTOWNARDS RD.

To Stormont & Newtownards

ROYAL AVE.

CASTLE

DONEGALL PL.

HIGH ST.

ANN ST.

QUEEN ELIZABETH BRIDGE

QUEENS BRIDGE

BRIDGE END

SHORT STRAND

MOUNT POTTINGER RD.

FOUNTAIN ST.

LINEN HALL LIBRARY

Donegall

VICTORIA SQUARE MALL

CHICHESTER ST.

OXFORD ST.

WATERFRONT HALL

MADRID ST.

CITY HALL

Square

BELFAST WHEEL

MAY ST.

EAST BRIDGE ST.

RAVENHILL RD.

ALBERT BRIDGE RD.

BEDFORD ST.

LINEN HALL

ADELAIDE ST.

ALFRED ST.

CROMAC ST.

ST. GEORGE'S MARKET

CENTRAL STATION

WOODSTOCK RD.

ORMEAU AVE.

MARYVILLE ST.

RAPHAEL ST.

STEWART ST.

See Central Belfast map

DONEGALL PASS

VERNON ST.

Botanic Station

CROMWELL RD.

WEST-MINSTER ST.

ORMEAU RD.

RIVER TERR.

BALFOUR AVE.

Lagan

UNIVERSITY

RUGBY RD.

UNIVERSITY AVE.

BALFOUR AVE.

River

EMBANKMENT ORMEAU

AGINCOURT AVE.

PALM HOUSE

RUGBY AVE.

Ormeau Park

Botanic Gardens

N

200 Meters

200 Yards

Minibus Tours—McComb's Antrim Coast Tour visits the Giant's Causeway, Dunluce Castle, the Carrick-a-Rede Rope Bridge, and Old Bushmills Distillery (£25, doesn't include distillery admission, daily 9:45–18:45 depending on demand, book through and depart from Belfast International City Hostel). They also have private guides (book in advance, tel. 028/9031-5333, www.minicoachni.co.uk). **Causeway Express,** run by the same company, zips you straight to the Giant's Causeway and back, giving you 2.5 hours at the Causeway to explore (£15, daily June–Aug, otherwise Sat–Sun only, departs at 11:00, returns to Belfast at 16:00).

Titanic Tours Belfast is run by former TV reporter Susie Millar, who is the great-granddaughter of a crew member on the fateful cruise. It's operated as a minivan tour (seats six) that picks up and drops off at your hotel. She spends half a day driving you around the major *Titanic* sights in Belfast, explaining them as you go. She is also available for longer, customized tours (£25, tel. 028/9065-9971, mobile 078-5271-6655, www .titanictours-belfast.co.uk, info@titanictours-belfast.co.uk).

Boat Tours—The Lagan Boat Company shows you shipyards on a 75-minute **Titanic Tour** cruise, narrated by a member of the Belfast Titanic Society. The tour shows off the fruits of the city's £800 million investment in its harbor, including a weir built to control the tides and stabilize the depth of the harbor (it doubles as a free pedestrian bridge over the River Lagan). The heart of the tour is a lazy harbor cruise past rusty dry-dock gates, brought alive by the guide's proud commentary and passed-around historical photos (£10; daily sailings at 12:30, 14:00, and 15:30; fewer off-season, tel. 028/9033-0844, mobile 077-1891-0423, www.laganboatcompany.com). Tours depart from the Lagan Pedestrian Bridge and Weir on Donegall Quay. The quay is located just past the leaning Albert Clock Tower, a five-minute walk from the TI.

Local Guide—Ken Harper has a vast knowledge of Belfast and does insightful tours from his taxi, focusing on both Catholic and Protestant neighborhoods, *Titanic*-related sights, and Belfast's favorite sons—author C. S. Lewis and musician Van Morrison. He's also available for custom tours, which he calls "Pick Ken's Brain" (£25 minimum or £8/person, 75 min, tel. 028/9074-2711, mobile 0771-175-7178, www.harpertaxitours.com, kenharper2004 @hotmail.com).

Sights in Belfast

Most sights of interest are located in three areas: the Catholic and Protestant neighborhoods to the west of the city center, central Belfast, and south Belfast.

Catholic and Protestant Neighborhoods

It will be a happy day when the sectarian neighborhoods of Belfast have nothing to be sectarian about. For a look at three of the original home bases of the Troubles, explore the working-class neighborhoods of Catholic Falls Road and Protestant Shankill Road (west of the Westlink motorway), or Protestant Sandy Row (south of the Westlink motorway).

Murals (found only in sectarian areas) are a memorable part of any visit to Belfast. But with more peaceful times, the character of these murals is changing. The Re-Imaging Communities Program has spent £3 million in government money to replace aggressive murals with positive ones. Paramilitary themes are being covered over with images of pride in each neighborhood's culture. The *Titanic* was built primarily by proud Protestant Ulster stock and is now seen more often in their neighborhood murals—reflecting their industrious work ethic. Over in the Catholic neighborhoods, you'll see more murals depicting mythological heroes from the days before the English came.

You can get tours of Falls Road or Shankill Road (see listings that follow), but rarely are both combined in one tour. Ken Harper is one of a new breed of Belfast taxi drivers who will give you an insightful private tour of both (see "Local Guide," previous page).

▲▲**Falls Road**—At the intersection of Castle and King Streets, you'll find the Castle Junction Car Park. This nine-story parking garage's basement (entrance on King Street) is filled with old black cabs—and the only Irish-language signs in downtown Belfast. These shared black cabs efficiently shuttle residents from outlying neighborhoods up and down Falls Road and to the city center. This service originated over 40 years ago at the beginning of the Troubles, when locals would hijack city buses and use them as barricades in the street fighting. When bus service was discontinued, local paramilitary groups established the shared taxi service. Although the buses are now running again, these cab rides are still a great value for their drivers' commentary.

Any cab goes up Falls Road, past Sinn Fein headquarters and lots of murals, to the Milltown Cemetery (£4, sit in front and talk to the cabbie). Hop in and out. Easy-to-flag-down cabs run every minute or so in each direction on Falls Road.

Forty trained cabbies do one-hour tours (minimum £30, £10/person for 90 min, £20/additional hour, cheap for a small group of up to 6 riders, tel. 028/9031-5777 or mobile 078-9271-6660, www.taxitrax.com).

The Sinn Fein office and bookstore are near the bottom of Falls Road. The bookstore is worth a look. Page through books featuring color photos of the political murals that decorated these buildings. Money raised here sup-

ports the families of deceased IRA members.

A sad, corrugated structure called the Peace Wall runs a block or so north of Falls Road (along Cupar Way), separating the Catholics from the Protestants in the Shankill Road area. This is just one of 17 such walls in Belfast.

At the Milltown Cemetery, walk past all the Gaelic crosses down to the far right-hand corner (closest to the highway), where

the IRA Roll of Honor is set apart from the thousands of other graves by little green railings. They are treated like fallen soldiers. Notice the memorial to Bobby Sands and nine other hunger strikers. They starved themselves to death in the nearby Maze prison in 1981, protesting for political prisoner status as opposed to terrorist criminal treat-

ment. The prison closed in the fall of 2000.

Shankill Road and Sandy Row—You can ride a shared black cab through the Protestant Shankill Road area (£25 for 1–2 people, £35 for 3–6 people, 60 min, tel. 028/9032-8775). Depart from North Street near the intersection with Millfield Road; it's not well-marked, but watch where the cabs circle and pick up locals on the south side of the street.

An easier (and cheaper) way to get a dose of the Unionist side is to walk Sandy Row. From Hotel Europa, walk a block down Glengall Street, then turn left for a 10-minute walk along a working-class Protestant street. A stop in the Unionist memorabilia shop, a pub, or one of the many cheap eateries here may give you an opportunity to talk to a local. You'll see murals filled with Unionist symbolism. The mural of William of Orange's victory over the Catholic King James II (Battle of the Boyne, 1690) thrills Unionist hearts.

Central Belfast

▲▲**City Hall**—This grand structure was closed in 2007 for renovation, and is due to reopen by January 2010. With its 173-foot-tall copper dome, it dominates the town center. Built between 1898 and 1906, with its statue of Queen Victoria scowling down Belfast's main drag and the Union Jack flapping behind her, the City Hall is a stirring sight. In the garden, you'll find memorials to the *Titanic* and the landing of the US Expeditionary Force in 1942—the first American troops to arrive in Europe en route to Berlin.

If it's open, take the free, 45-minute tour (June–Sept usually Mon–Fri at 11:00, 14:00, and 15:00, Sat at 14:00 and 15:00; Oct–May Mon–Fri at 11:00 and 14:30, Sat only at 14:30; no tours on Sun; enter at the front of the building except on Sat, when you enter at the back on the south side; call to check schedule and to reserve, tel. 028/9027-0456, www.belfastcity.gov.uk /cityhall). The tour gives you a rundown on city government and an explanation of the decor that makes this an Ulster political hall of fame. Queen Victoria and King Edward VII look down on city council meetings. The 1613 original charter of Belfast granted by James I is on display. Its Great Hall—bombed by the Germans in 1941—looks as great as it did the day it was made.

If you can't manage a tour, but the City Hall is open, at least step inside, admire the marble swirl staircase, and drop into the "What's on in Belfast" room just inside the front door.

Belfast Wheel—City Hall is now flanked by an equally tall, "temporary" observation wheel similar to London's Eye. A ride in one of this Ferris wheel's 42 enclosed capsules offers views over Belfast and Belfast Lough (may become permanent, £6.50, daily 10:00–21:00).

Linen Hall Library—Across the street from City Hall, the 200-year-old Linen Hall Library welcomes guests (notice the red hand above the main front door facing Donegall Square North; see "The Red Hand of Ulster" sidebar, later in this chapter). Described

BELFAST

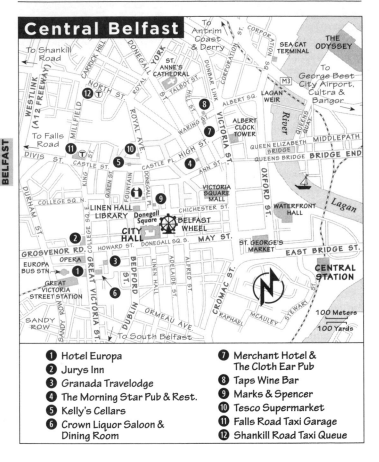

Central Belfast

1. Hotel Europa
2. Jurys Inn
3. Granada Travelodge
4. The Morning Star Pub & Rest.
5. Kelly's Cellars
6. Crown Liquor Saloon & Dining Room
7. Merchant Hotel & The Cloth Ear Pub
8. Taps Wine Bar
9. Marks & Spencer
10. Tesco Supermarket
11. Falls Road Taxi Garage
12. Shankill Road Taxi Queue

as "Ulster's attic," the library takes pride in being a neutral space where anyone trying to make sense of the sectarian conflict can view the Troubled Images, a historical collection of engrossing political posters. It has a fine hardbound ambience, a coffee shop, and a royal newspaper reading room (Mon–Fri 9:30–17:30, Sat 9:30–16:00, closed Sun, get free visitor's pass at entrance on Fountain Street, 17 Donegall Square North, tel. 028/9032-1707, www.linenhall.com).

Golden Mile—This is the overstated nickname of Belfast's liveliest dining and entertainment district, which stretches from the Opera House (Great Victoria Street) to the university (University Road).

The **Grand Opera House,** originally built in 1895, bombed and rebuilt in 1991, and bombed and rebuilt again in 1993, is extravagantly Victorian and *the* place to take in a concert, play, or opera (£3, guided tours Wed–Sat at 11:00; ticket office open Mon–

Fri 9:00–20:00, Sat 10:00–15:00, closed Sun; ticket office to right of main front door on Great Victoria Street, tel. 028/9024-1919, www.goh.co.uk). The recommended **Hotel Europa,** next door, while considered the most-bombed hotel in the world, feels pretty casual but is expensive to stay in.

Across the street is the museum-like **Crown Liquor Saloon.** Built in 1849, it's now a part of the National Trust. A wander through its mahogany, glass, and marble interior is a trip back into the day of Queen Victoria, although the privacy provided by the snugs—booths—allows for un-Victorian behavior (Mon–Sat 11:30–24:00, Sun 12:30–23:00, consider a lunch stop, see listing under "Eating in Belfast," later). Upstairs, the Crown Dining Room serves pub grub, is decorated with historic photos, and is the starting point for a pub walk (see "Tours in Belfast").

The Odyssey—This huge millennium-project complex offers a food pavilion, bowling alley, and **W5,** a science center with stimulating, interactive exhibits for youngsters. Where else can a kid play a harp with laser-light strings? The name W5 stands for who, what, when, where, and why (£7, kids-£5, Mon–Thu 10:00–19:00, Fri–Sat 10:00–20:00, Sun 12:00–18:00, tel. 028/9046-7700, www.w5online.co.uk). There's also a 12-screen cinema and a 10,000-seat arena where the Belfast Giants professional ice hockey team skates from September to April (2 Queen's Quay, 10-min walk from Central Station, tel. 028/9045-1055, www.theodyssey.co.uk).

South Belfast

▲Ulster Museum—While mediocre by European standards, this is Belfast's one major museum; however, it's closed for renovation until early 2010.

When open, the museum is free and pretty painless. Ride the elevator to the top floor and follow the spiraling exhibits downhill; there's a cheery café halfway down. You'll find an interesting *Made in Belfast* exhibit just before an arch that proclaims, "Trade is the golden girdle of the globe." The delicately worded history section is given an interesting British slant (such as the implication that the Great Potato Famine of 1845 was caused by the Irish population doubling in 40 years—without a mention of various English contributions to the suffering). After a peek at a pretty good mummy, top things off with the *Girona* treasure. Soggy bits of gold, silver, leather, and wood were salvaged from the Spanish Armada's shipwrecked *Girona,* lost off the Antrim Coast north of Belfast in 1588 (free, likely Mon–Fri 10:00–17:00, Sat 13:00–17:00,

Sun 14:00–17:00, in Botanic Gardens on Stranmillis Road, south of downtown, tel. 028/9038-3000, www.ulstermuseum.org.uk).

▲Botanic Gardens—This is the backyard of Queen's University, and on a sunny day, you couldn't imagine a more relaxing park setting. On a cold day, step into the Tropical Ravine for a jungle of heat and humidity. Take a quick walk through the Palm House, reminiscent of the one in London's Kew Gardens but smaller (free, Mon–Fri 10:00–12:00 & 13:00–17:00, Sat–Sun 13:00–17:00, shorter hours in winter; gardens open daily 8:00 until dusk, tel. 028/9031-4762, www.belfastcity.gov.uk/parks). The Ulster Museum is on the grounds.

Near Belfast

▲▲Ulster Folk and Transport Museum—This 180-acre, two-museum complex straddles the road and rail at Cultra, midway between Bangor and Belfast (eight miles east of town).

The Folk Museum, an open-air collection of 34 reconstructed buildings from all over the nine counties of Ulster, showcases the region's traditional lifestyles. After wandering through the old-town site (church, print shop, schoolhouse, humble Belfast row house, silent movie theater, and so on), you'll head off into the country to nip into cottages, farmhouses, and mills. Most houses are warmed by a wonderful peat fire and a friendly attendant. It can be dull or vibrant, depending upon when you visit and your ability to chat with the attendants. Drop a peat brick on the fire.

The Transport Museum (downhill, over the road from the folk section) consists of three buildings. Start at the bottom and

 trace the evolution of transportation from 7,500 years ago—when people first decided to load an ox—to the first vertical take-off jet. The lowest building holds an intriguing section on the sinking of the Belfast-made *Titanic*. Nearby are exhibits on the Belfast-based Shorts aircraft company, which partnered with the Wright Brothers to manufacture the first commercially available aircraft in 1909. Two other buildings cover the history of bikes, cars, and trains. The car section rumbles from the first car in Ireland (an 1898 Benz) through the "Cortina Culture" of the 1960s to the local adventures of controversial John DeLorean and a 1981 model of his car.

Cost, Hours, Location: £5.50 for Folk Museum, £5.50 for Transport Museum, £7 combo-ticket for both, £19 for families;

The Red Hand of Ulster

All over Belfast, you'll notice a curious symbol: a red hand facing you as if swearing a pledge or telling you to halt. You'll spot it above the Linen Hall Library door, in the wrought-iron fences of the Merchant Hotel, on old-fashioned clothes wringers (in the Ulster Folk and Transport Museum at Cultra), above the front door of a bank in Bangor, in the shape of a flowerbed at Mount Stewart House, in Loyalist paramilitary murals, on shield emblems in the gates of Republican memorials, and even on the flag of Northern Ireland (the white flag with the red cross of St. George). It's known as the Red Hand of Ulster—and it seems to pop up everywhere. Although it's more often associated with Unionist traditions, it's one of the few emblems used by both communities in Northern Ireland.

Nationalists display the red-hand-on-a-yellow-shield as a symbol of the ancient province of Ulster. It was the official crest of the once-dominant O'Neill clan (who fought tooth and nail against English rule) and today signifies resistance to British rule in these communities.

But you'll more often see the red hand in Unionist areas. They see it as a potent symbol of the political entity of Northern Ireland. The Ulster Volunteer Force chose it for their symbol in 1913 and embedded it in the center of the Northern Irish flag upon partition of the island in 1921. You'll often see the red hand clenched as a fist in Loyalist murals.

The origin of the red hand comes from a mythological tale of two rival clans that raced by boat to claim a far shore. The first clan leader to touch the shore would win it for his people. Everyone aboard both vessels strained mightily at their oars, near exhaustion as they approached the shore. Finally, in desperation, the chieftain leader of the slower boat whipped out his sword and lopped off his right hand...which he then flung onto the shore, thus winning the coveted land. Moral of the story? The fearless folk of Ulster will do *whatever* it takes to get the job done.

July–Sept Mon–Sat 10:00–18:00, Sun 11:00–18:00; March–June Mon–Fri 10:00–17:00, Sat 10:00–18:00, Sun 11:00–18:00; Oct–Feb closes daily at 16:00. Check the schedule for the day's special events (tel. 028/9042-8428, www.uftm.org.uk). Allow three hours for your visit, and expect lots of walking. Those with a car can drive from one section to the next.

From Belfast, you can reach **Cultra** by taxi (£10), bus #502

(2/hr, 30 min from Laganside Bus Centre), or train (£4 round-trip, 2/hr, 15 min, from any Belfast train station or from Bangor). Trains and buses stop right in the park, but train service is more dependable. Public-transport schedules are skimpy on Saturday and Sunday.

Carrickfergus Castle—Built during the Norman invasion of the late 1100s, this historic castle stands sentry on the shore of Belfast Lough. William of Orange landed here in 1690, when he began his Irish campaign against deposed King James II. In 1778, the American privateer ship *Ranger* (first ever to fly the stars-and-stripes flag), under the command of John Paul Jones, defeated the more heavily armed HMS *Drake* just offshore.

These days the castle feels a bit sanitized and geared for kids, but it's an easy excursion if you're seeking a castle experience near the city. If arriving by train, turn left as you exit the train station and walk straight downhill for five minutes—all the way to the waterfront—passing under the arch of the old town wall en route. You'll find the castle on your right (£3; April–Sept Mon–Sat 10:00–18:00, Sun 12:00–18:00; Oct–March Mon–Sat 10:00–16:00, Sun 14:00–16:00; last entry 30 min before closing, 20-min train ride from Belfast on line to Larne costs £3.50 round-trip, tel. 028/9335-1273).

Sleeping in Belfast

South Belfast

Many of Belfast's best budget beds cluster in a comfortable, leafy neighborhood of row houses just south of Queen's University (and the Ulster Museum). Two train stations (Botanic and Adelaide) are nearby, and buses (£1.50) zip down Malone Road every 20 minutes. Any bus on Malone Road goes to Donegall Square East. Taxis take you downtown for about £4 (your host can call one).

$$$ Malone Lodge Hotel, by far the classiest listing in this neighborhood, provides slick, business-class comfort in 84 spacious rooms on a quiet street (Db-£85–150, superior Db-£120–175, weekend deals, elevator, Wi-Fi, restaurant, 60 Eglantine Avenue, tel. 028/9038-8000, fax 028/9038-8088, www.malonelodgehotel.com, info@malonelodgehotel.com).

$$ Camera Guest House rents 10 smoke-free rooms and has an airy, hardwood feeling throughout (S-£36, Ss-£45, Sb-£50,

Sleep Code

(£1 = about $1.60; country code: 44, area code: 028)
To call Belfast from the Republic of Ireland, dial 048 before the local 8-digit number.
S = Single, **D** = Double/Twin, **T** = Triple, **Q** = Quad, **b** = bathroom, **s** = shower only. Unless otherwise noted, breakfast is included and credit cards are accepted.

To help you easily sort through these listings, I've divided the rooms into three categories, based on the price for a double room with bath:

$$$ Higher Priced—Most rooms £90 or more.
$$ Moderately Priced—Most rooms between £60–90.
$ Lower Priced—Most rooms £60 or less.

Ds-£58, Db-£65, family room-£82, 44 Wellington Park, tel. 028/9066-0026, fax 028/9066-7856, www.cameraguesthouse.com, camera_gh@hotmail.com, Bronagh and Peter).

$$ Malone Guest House is a crisp, stand-alone Victorian house fronting the busy Malone Road. It's homey and well-run by Geraldine and Byron Quinn, who rent 13 prim rooms (Sb-£35–50, Db-£60–65, Tb-£70–80, 79 Malone Road, at intersection with Adelaide Park and bus stop, tel. 028/9066-9565, fax 028/9037-5090, www.maloneguesthousebelfast.co.uk, maloneguesthouse belfast@yahoo.co.uk).

$ Windermere Guest House has 11 rooms, including several small-but-pleasant singles, in a large Victorian house (S-£31, Sb-£42, D-£56, Db-£60, T-£70, cash only, 60 Wellington Park, tel. 028/9066-2693, www.windermereguesthouse.co.uk, windermere guesthouse@ntlworld.com).

Eglantine Avenue B&Bs: On the same quiet street (Eglantine Avenue), you'll find these two basic budget choices: **$$ Marine House B&B,** set back from the road, is a grand old place with 10 high-ceilinged rooms (Sb-£47, Db-£60–65, Tb-£85, Qb-£100, at #30, Wi-Fi, parking, tel. & fax 028/9066-2828, www.marine guesthouse3star.com, marine30@utvinternet.co.uk) and **$ The George B&B,** with six average, smallish rooms (S-£40, Db-£55, Tb-£80, at #9, tel. 028/9068-3212, georgeguesthouse@hotmail .com).

Hotels

Belfast is more of a business town than a tourist town, so business-class room rates are lower or soft on weekends (best prices booked from their websites).

In Central Belfast

$$$ Hotel Europa is Belfast's landmark hotel—fancy, comfortable, and central—with four stars and good weekend rates. Modern yet elegant, this place was Clinton's choice when he visited (Db-£140–220 plus £16 breakfast, President Clinton's suite-£400, 7 non-smoking floors, Great Victoria Street, tel. 028/9027-1066, fax 028/9032-7800, www.hastingshotels.com, res@eur.hastings hotels.com).

$$$ Jurys Inn, an American-style place that rents its 190 identical modern rooms for one simple price, is perfectly located two blocks from City Hall (up to 3 adults or 2 adults and 2 kids for £69–120, breakfast-£10 extra/person, all non-smoking, Fisherwick Place, tel. 028/9053-3500, fax 028/9053-3511, www.jurysinns.com, jurysinnbelfast@jurysinns.com).

$$ Granada Travelodge, quiet and extremely central, is a basic Jurys-style business hotel with 90 cookie-cutter rooms high on value, but low on character (Db-£59–109, a block from Hotel Europa and City Hall at 15 Brunswick Street, reservations toll tel. 087/1984-6188, fax 028/9023-2999, www.travelodge.ie).

Near Queen's University

$$$ Wellington Park Hotel is a dependable, chain-style hotel with 75 rooms. It's predictable but in a good location (Db-£132 weekdays, Db-£105 weekends, Wi-Fi, parking, 21 Malone Road, tel. 028/9038-1111, fax 028/9066-5410, www.wellington parkhotel.com, info@wellingtonparkhotel.com).

$$ Belfast Holiday Inn Express, not as central as other hotels (a 10-minute walk east of Queens University), offers the same basic formula (Db-£75–95, kids free, includes breakfast, all non-smoking, elevator, by Botanic Station at 106A University Street, tel. 028/9031-1909, fax 028/9031-1910, www.exhi-belfast .com, mail@exhi-belfast.com).

$$ Benedicts Hotel, with a local feel, has 32 rooms in a good location at the northern fringe of the Queen's University district. Its popular bar is a maze of polished wood and can be loud on weekend nights (Sb-£70-75, Db-£80–90, elevator, 7–21 Bradbury Place, tel. 028/9059-1999, fax 028/9059-1990, www.benedicts hotel.co.uk, info@benedictshotel.co.uk).

Hostels and Dorms

$ Belfast International City Hostel, providing the best value among Belfast's hostels with its 200 beds, is big and creatively run. It offers single and double rooms along with dorms, and is located near Botanic Station, in the heart of the lively university district and close to the center. Features include free lockers, elevator, baggage storage, pay Internet access and Wi-Fi,

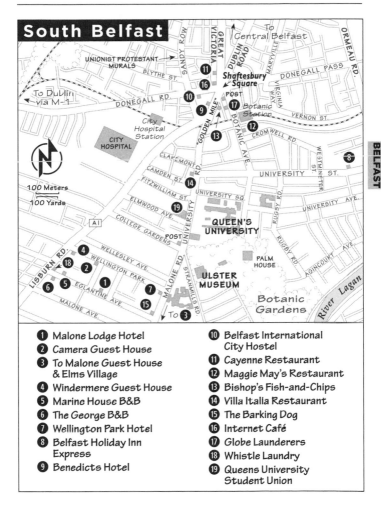

South Belfast

1. Malone Lodge Hotel
2. Camera Guest House
3. To Malone Guest House & Elms Village
4. Windermere Guest House
5. Marine House B&B
6. The George B&B
7. Wellington Park Hotel
8. Belfast Holiday Inn Express
9. Benedicts Hotel
10. Belfast International City Hostel
11. Cayenne Restaurant
12. Maggie May's Restaurant
13. Bishop's Fish-and-Chips
14. Villa Italia Restaurant
15. The Barking Dog
16. Internet Café
17. Globe Launderers
18. Whistle Laundry
19. Queens University Student Union

kitchen, self-serve laundry (£3.50), a cheap breakfast-only cafeteria, 24-hour reception, and no curfew (bed in 6-bed dorm-£10, bed in quad-£12, S-£22, D-£28–31, Db-£37, 22–32 Donegall Road, tel. 028/9031-5435, fax 028/9043-9699, www.hini.org .uk, info@hini.org.uk). Paul, the manager of the hostel, is a veritable TI, with a passion for his work. The hostel is the starting point for **McComb's** mini-bus tours (described earlier in "Tours in Belfast").

$ Elms Village, a huge Queen's University dorm complex, rents 100 basic, institutional rooms (singles only) to travelers during summer break (mid-June–early-Sept only, Sb-£41, includes breakfast, cheaper for students, coin-op laundry, self-serve kitchen; reception building is 50 yards down entry street, marked *Elms*

Village on low brick wall, 78 Malone Road; tel. 028/9097-4525, fax 028/9097-4524, www.qub.ac.uk, accommodation@qub .ac.uk).

Eating in Belfast

Downtown

If it's £12 pub grub you want, consider these drinking holes with varied atmospheres.

The Morning Star is woody and elegant (£9–15 restaurant dinners upstairs, £5 buffet Mon–Sat 12:00–16:00, open daily 12:00–21:00, Thu–Sat until 22:00, down alley just off High Street at 17 Pottinger's Entry, roughly opposite the post office, tel. 028/9023-5986).

Kelly's Cellars—once a rebel hangout (see plaque above door)—still has a very Irish feel. It's 300 years old and hard to find, but worth it (Mon–Sat 11:30–24:30, Sun 13:00–23:30, live traditional music nightly at 21:30 and Sat at 16:30, 32 Bank Street, 100 yards behind Tesco supermarket, access via alley on left side when facing Tesco, tel. 028/9024-6058).

Crown Liquor Saloon, a recommended stop along the Golden Mile (described earlier under "Sights in Belfast") is small and antique. Its mesmerizing mishmash of mosaics and shareable snugs—booths—are topped with a smoky tin ceiling (Mon–Sat lunch only 11:30–15:00, Sun 12:00–17:00, 46 Great Victoria Street, across from Hotel Europa, tel. 028/9024-3187). The **Crown Dining Room** upstairs offers dependable £9–13 meals (Mon–Sat 12:00–21:00, Sun 16:00–21:00, tel. 028/9024-3187, use entry on Amelia Street when the Crown Liquor Saloon is closed).

Supermarkets: **Marks & Spencer** has a coffee shop serving skinny lattes, and a supermarket in its basement (Mon–Sat 9:00–19:00, Thu until 21:00, Sun 13:00–18:00, WCs on second floor, Donegall Place, a block north of Donegall Square). **Tesco,** another supermarket, is a block north of Marks & Spencer, and two blocks north of Donegall Square (Mon–Sat 8:00–19:00, Thu until 21:00, Sun 13:00–17:00, Royal Avenue and Bank Street). Picnic on the City Hall green.

In the Cathedral Quarter

I like the cluster of culture surrounding the Cotton Court section of Waring Street. It's about a 10-minute walk northeast of the City Hall.

Check out the lobby of **Merchant Hotel** (a grand former bank) for a glimpse of crushed-velvet Victorian splendor under an opulent dome, and consider indulging Belfast's best afternoon tea splurge. Don't show up in shorts and Birkenstocks (£17.50 tea, daily 12:00–17:00, 35–39 Waring Street, tel. 028/9023-4888).

Taps Wine Bar is a whiff of Mediterranean warmth in a cold brick city. Try a cheerful tapas or paella meal washed down with sangria (May–Sept daily 12:00–22:00; Oct–April closed Sun; 42 Waring Street, tel. 028/9031-1414).

The Cloth Ear is a friendly modern bar serving better-than-average pub grub that comes from the kitchen of the posh Merchant Hotel next door. Irish music sessions are a Sunday afternoon tradition starting at 15:00 (Mon–Sat 12:00–21:00, Sun 13:00–19:00, tel. 028/9026-2719).

Near Shaftesbury Square and Botanic Station

Nearby Queens University gives this neighborhood an energetic feel, with a mixed bag of dining options ranging from cosmopolitan to deep-fried.

Cayenne is a trendy-yet-friendly restaurant refuge hiding behind Belfast's most understated exterior. It's your best bet for gourmet food—innovative global cuisine—without a snobby attitude. Owner Paul Rankin stars in the *Ready Steady Cook* TV show on BBC (£15–22 meals, Tue–Fri 12:00–14:30 & 17:00–22:00, Sat 18:00–23:00, Sun 17:00–21:00, closed Mon; £16 three-course lunch; early-bird specials before 18:45: £20 for two courses or £25 for three courses at dinner; reservations smart on weekends; Shaftesbury Square at 7 Ascot House—look for plain, gray, blocky slab front; tel. 028/9033-1532).

Maggie May's serves hearty, simple, cheap £7–10 meals (Mon–Sat 8:00–22:30, Sun 10:00–22:30, one block south of Botanic Station at 50 Botanic Avenue, tel. 028/9032-2662).

Bishop's is the locals' choice for fish-and-chips (daily 12:00–23:30, pasta and veggie options, classier side has table service, just south of Shaftesbury Square at Bradbury Place, tel. 028/9043-9070).

Villa Italia packs in crowds hungry for linguini and *bistecca*. With its checkered tablecloths and a wood-beamed ceiling draped with grape leaves, it's a little bit of Italy in Belfast (£9–15 meals, Mon–Fri 17:00–23:00, Sat–Sun 16:00–23:00, 39 University Road, 3 long blocks south of Shaftesbury Square, at intersection with University Street, tel. 028/9032-8356).

The Barking Dog is closest to my cluster of B&B listings south of Queen's University. It's a hip grill serving tasty beef burgers, duck, scallops, and other filling fare. If the weather's fine, the tree-shaded front deck is ideal for people-watching (£6–9 lunches, £10–15 dinners, daily 12:00–22:00, Sat–Sun brunch 10:00–16:00, near corner of Eglantine Avenue at 33–35 Malone Road, tel. 028/9066-1885).

Belfast Connections

For updated schedules and prices for both trains and buses in Northern Ireland, check with Translink (tel. 028/9066-6630, www.translink.co.uk). Consider a £15 "Day Tracker" ticket, good for all-day train and bus use in Northern Ireland. Service is less frequent on Sundays.

From Belfast by Train to: Dublin (8/day, 5/day Sun, 2 hrs), **Derry** (9/day, 2.5 hrs), **Larne** (hourly, 1 hr), **Portrush** (11/day, 5/day Sun, 2 hrs, transfer in Coleraine). Train info: tel. 028/9066-6630.

By Bus to: Portrush (12/day, 2 hrs, £8, scenic-coast route, 2.5 hrs), **Derry** (20/day, 1.75 hrs), **Dublin** (hourly, most via Dublin Airport, 2.75–3 hrs), **Glasgow** (3/day, 5.75 hrs), **Edinburgh** (3/day, 7 hrs). The Europa Bus Centre is behind Hotel Europa (Ulsterbus tel. 028/9033-7003 for destinations in Scotland and England, tel. 028/9066-6630 for destinations in Northern Ireland).

By Plane: Belfast has two airports. George Best Belfast City Airport (www.belfastcityairport.com) is a five-minute taxi ride from town (near the docks), while Belfast International Airport (www.belfastairport.com) is 18 miles west of town, connected by buses from the Europa Bus Centre behind the Europa Hotel. There are cheap flights to **Glasgow,** Scotland, on easyJet (www .easyjet.com) and Flybe (www.flybe.com); and flights to **London**'s Heathrow Airport on bmi (www.flybmi.com).

By Bus to Dublin Airport: Aircoach buses depart from Jurys Inn Hotel in Belfast (hourly, 6:30–20:30, 2.5 hrs, £15 one-way, www.aircoach.ie).

By Ferry to Scotland: There are a number of options, ports, and companies. You can sail between Belfast and **Stranraer** on the Stena Line ferry (4–6/ day, 2–3.25 hrs, £25, tel. 028/9074-7747, www.stena line.co.uk).

P&O Ferry (toll tel. 0870-2424-777, www.poirish sea.com) goes from **Larne** (20 miles north of Belfast, hourly trains, 1-hr trip, TI tel. 028/2826-0088) to **Cairnryan** (10/day, 1 hr) or to **Troon** (2/day, 2 hrs).

By Ferry to England: You can sail from Belfast to **Birkenhead** (10 min from Liverpool) on Norfolkline Irish Sea Ferries (daily at 10:30 and 22:30, 8 hrs, fares can include meals and a cabin, toll tel. 0844-847-5042, www.norfolkline-ferries.co.uk).

Bangor

To stay in a laid-back seaside hometown—with more comfort per pound—sleep 30 minutes east of Belfast in Bangor (BANG-grr). It's a handy alternative for travelers who find Belfast booked up by occasional conventions and conferences. Formerly a Victorian resort and Belfast seaside escape, Bangor now has a sleepy and almost residential feeling. But with

elegant old homes facing its spruced-up harbor and the lack of even a hint of big-city Belfast, Bangor has appeal. The harbor is a 10-minute walk from the train station.

To visit two worthwhile sights near Bangor—the Somme Heritage Centre and Mount Stewart House—consider renting a car for the day at George Best Belfast City Airport, a 15-minute train trip from Bangor.

Getting There

Catch the train from Belfast Central to Bangor (2/hr, 30 min, go to the end of the line—don't get off at Bangor West). Before 9:30 it's £4.60 one-way or £7.20 for a same-day round-trip (after 9:30 it's only £4.80 round-trip). Consider stopping en route at Cultra (Ulster Folk and Transport Museum; see listing under "Sights in Belfast," earlier). The journey gives you a good close-up look at the giant Belfast harbor cranes.

If day-tripping into Belfast from Bangor, get off at Belfast Central (free shuttle bus to the town center, 4/hr, not Sun), or stay on until Botanic Station for the Ulster Museum, the Golden Mile, and Sandy Row.

Orientation to Bangor

Bangor's **TI** is at 34 Quay Street (July–Aug Mon–Fri 9:00–18:00, Sat 10:00–17:00, Sun 13:00–17:00; Sept–June Mon–Fri 9:00–17:00; Sat 10:00–17:00, closed Sun; tel. 028/9127-0069). You'll find **Sud's Launderette** on Southwell Road facing the harbor (Mon–Sat 8:00–18:00, closed Sun, tel. 028/9145-6546). You can get free Internet access at the **library** on Hamilton Road (30-min limit).

Sights in Bangor

For sightseeing, your time is better spent in Belfast. But if you have time to burn in Bangor, enjoy a walk next to the water on the **Coastal Path** leading west out of town from the marina.

For a shorter walk with views of the marina, head to the end of the **North Pier,** where you'll find a mosaic honoring the D-Day fleet that rendezvoused offshore in 1944, far from Nazi reconnaissance aircraft. Keep an eye out in the marina for Rose the seal.

You can glean some local Viking history at the **North Down Museum,** behind the Town Hall on the grassy grounds uphill and opposite the train station (free, Tue–Sat 10:00–16:30, Sun 14:00–16:30, closed Mon, tel. 028/9127-1200).

Sleeping in Bangor

(£1 = about $1.60, country code: 44, area code: 028)
Visitors arriving in Bangor (by train) come down Main Street to reach the harbor marina. You'll find my first two listings to the right, along the waterfront east of the marina on Seacliff Road. The other two listings are to the left, just uphill and west of the marina.

$$ Salty Dog Hotel is a freshly renovated relic with a grand brick facade, 15 comfortable and well-appointed rooms, and a ground-floor bistro (Db-£60–90, Tb-£90–105, 10–12 Seacliff Road near the base of the North Pier, tel. 028/9127-0696, www .thesaltydogbangor.com).

$$ Hargreaves House, a homey Victorian waterfront refuge, is Bangor's best value and has three cozy rooms (S-£35–45, Sb-£40–50, D-£60, Db-£60–80, non-smoking, 78 Seacliff Road, 10 percent discount with cash and 2-night stay—only with 2010 edition of this book in hand upon arrival, online discounts, Wi-Fi, 15-min walk from train station but worth it, tel. 028/9146-4071, mobile 079-8058-5047, www.hargreaveshouse.com, info @hargreaveshouse.com, Pauline Mendez).

$$ Shelleven House is an old-fashioned, well-kept place with 11 prim rooms on the quiet corner of Princetown Road and Tennyson Avenue (Sb-£38–45, Db-£70–80, Tb-£85, all non-smoking, 61 Princetown Road, tel. 028/9127-1777, www.shelleven house.com, shellevenhouse@aol.com).

$ Bramble Lodge is closest to the train station (5-min walk), offering three inviting rooms (Sb-£35–40, Db-£55–60, non-smoking, 1 Bryansburn Road, tel. 028/9145-7924, jacquihanna _bramblelodge@yahoo.co.uk).

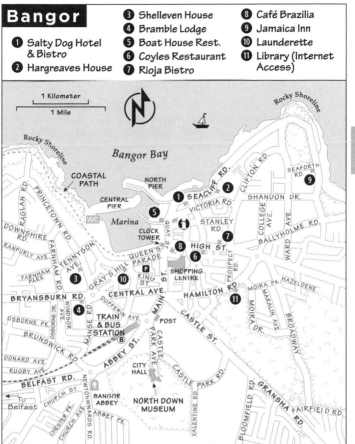

Bangor

1 Salty Dog Hotel & Bistro
2 Hargreaves House
3 Shelleven House
4 Bramble Lodge
5 Boat House Rest.
6 Coyles Restaurant
7 Rioja Bistro
8 Café Brazilia
9 Jamaica Inn
10 Launderette
11 Library (Internet Access)

BELFAST

Eating in Bangor

Habitually late diners should be aware that most restaurants in town close at 21:00 and stop seating at about 20:30.

The **Boat House** is a stout stone structure hiding the finest dining experience in Bangor. It's run by two Dutch brothers who specialize in some of the freshest fish dishes in Northern Ireland. Their £18 early-bird two-course meal or £21.50 three-course special, offered before 19:30, are great values (Mon–Sat 12:00–21:00, Sun 12:00–20:00, reserve ahead, on Sea Cliff Road opposite the TI, tel. 028/9146-9253).

Coyles has two floors of fun. Upstairs is a classy, jazzy restaurant serving £13–18 dinners (Tue–Sun 17:00–21:00, closed Mon), while downstairs is a comfy bar with dependable pub grub (daily

12:00–15:00 & 17:00–21:00, 44 High Street, tel. 028/9127-0362).

Rioja does Mediterranean bistro dishes served by an easy-going staff (Tue–Sat 17:00–21:00, lunches Fri–Sat 12:00–14:00, closed Sun–Mon, 119 High Street, tel. 028/9147-0774).

The **Salty Dog Bistro** has a stylish ambience and quality fare (Mon–Sat 12:00–21:00, Sun 12:00–20:00, near the base of the North Pier at 10–12 Seacliff Road, tel. 028/9127-0696).

Café Brazilia, a popular hangout at lunch, is across from the stubby clock tower (Mon–Fri 8:30–20:30, Sat 8:30–16:30, closed Sun, 13 Bridge Street, tel. 028/9127-2763).

The **Jamaica Inn** offers pleasant pub grub with a breezy waterfront porch (food served from about 12:00–21:00, 10-min walk east of the TI on Seacliff Road, 188 Seacliff Road, tel. 028/9147-1610).

Near Bangor

The eastern fringe of Northern Ireland is populated mostly by people who consider themselves true-blue British citizens with a history of loyalty to the crown that goes back over 400 years. Two sights within reach by car from Bangor highlight this area's firm roots in British culture: the Somme Heritage Centre and Mount Stewart House.

Getting There

Although patchy bus service can be used to reach these sights from Bangor (check with Bangor TI), I'd instead rent a car at George Best Belfast City Airport, which is only 15 minutes by train from Bangor or 10 minutes from Belfast Central train station. Since the airport is east of Belfast, your drive to these rural sights skips the headache of urban Belfast. Call ahead to confirm sight opening hours.

Somme Heritage Centre

World War I's trench warfare was a meat grinder, and Northern Ireland's men were not spared—especially during the bloody Battle of the Somme in France in July 1916. Among the Allied forces was the British Army's 36th Ulster Division, which drew heavily from this loyal heartland of Northern Ireland. Working-class soldiers and aristocrat officers alike hoped that their sacrifice in Britain's cause would prove their loyalty—and ensure that Ireland would remain British after the war (a Home Rule bill passed just before the war suggested the opposite would be the case). The 36th Ulster Division suffered brutal loses at the Battle of the Somme—of the 760 men recruited from the Shankill Road area in Belfast, only 10 percent survived.

Exhibits portray the battle experience through a mix of military artifacts, photos, and life-size figures posed in trench warfare re-creations. It's moving, but it can only hint at the horrific conditions endured by these soldiers. Guided tours go hourly on the hour (£5, July–Aug Mon–Fri 10:00–17:00, Sat–Sun 12:00–17:00; April–June and Sept Mon–Thu 10:00–16:00, Sat 12:00–16:00, closed Fri and Sun; Oct–March Mon–Thu 10:00–16:00, closed Fri–Sun; 233 Bangor Road, 3 miles south of Bangor just off the A-21, tel. 028/9182-3214, www.irishsoldier.org).

Mount Stewart House

No manor house in Ireland better illuminates the affluent lifestyle of the Protestant ascendancy than this lush estate. After the defeat

of James II (the last Catholic king of England) at the Battle of the Boyne in 1690, the Protestant monarchy was in control—and the privileged status of landowners of the same faith was assured. In the 1700s, Ireland's Catholic rebellion seemed finally to be squashed, so Anglican landlords felt safe flaunting their wealth in manor houses surrounded by utterly perfect gardens. The Mount Stewart House in particular was designed to dazzle.

Hourly tours give you a glimpse of the cushy life led by the Marques of Londonderry and his heirs over the past three centuries. The main entry hall is a stunner, with a black-and-white checkerboard tile floor, marble columns, classical statues, and pink walls supporting a balcony with a domed ceiling and a fine chandelier. You'll see the original seats occupied by the rears of European heads of state at the Congress of Vienna after Napoleon's 1815 defeat. A huge painting of "Hambletonian," a prize-winning racehorse, hangs above the grand staircase, dwarfing a portrait of the Duke of Wellington in a hall nearby. The heroic duke (worried that his Irish birth would be seen as lower class by British blue-bloods) once quipped, "Just because one is born in a stable does not make him a horse."

Afterwards, wander the expansive manicured gardens. The fantasy life of parasol-toting, upper-crust Victorian society seems to ooze from every viewpoint. Fanciful sculptures of extinct dodo birds and monkeys holding vases on their heads set off predictably classic Italian and Spanish sections. An Irish harp has been trimmed out of a hedge a few feet from a flowerbed shaped like the Red Hand of Ulster. Swans glide serenely among the lily pads on

a small lake (£7.40 for house and gardens, £5.60 gardens only; July–Aug daily 12:00–18:00; May–June and Sept Wed–Mon 13:00–18:00, closed Tue; April and Oct Thu–Sun 12:00–18:00, closed Mon–Wed; March Sat–Sun 12:00–18:00, closed weekdays; closed Nov–Feb; 8 miles south of Bangor, just off the A-20 beside Strangford Lough, tel. 028/4278-8387, www.nationaltrust. org.uk).

PORTRUSH AND THE ANTRIM COAST

The Antrim Coast—the north of Northern Ireland—is one of the most interesting and scenic coastlines in Ireland. Portrush, at the end of the train line, is an ideal base for exploring the highlights of the Antrim Coast. Within a few miles of the train terminal, you can visit evocative castle ruins, tour the world's oldest whiskey distillery, risk your life on a bouncy rope bridge, and hike along the famous Giant's Causeway.

Planning Your Time

You need a full day to explore the Antrim Coast, so allow two nights in Portrush. An ideal day could lace together Dunluce Castle, Old Bushmills Distillery, and the Giant's Causeway, followed by nine holes on the Portrush pitch-and-putt course.

Getting Around the Antrim Coast

By Bus: In July and August, a couple of all-day bus passes are available to help you get around the region economically. The better option is the £5 **Bushmills Open Topper,** connecting Portrush, Old Bushmills Distillery, and the Giant's Causeway every two hours. The £4.10 **Causeway Rambler**—which links Old Bushmills Distillery, the Giant's Causeway, and the Carrick-a-Rede Rope Bridge hourly—is less convenient because it doesn't include Portrush in its circuit (to get from Portrush to Bushmills, take a £8 taxi; those who want to see the rope bridge, along with the other sights, could consider getting both bus passes). For either pass, pick up a schedule at the TI and buy the ticket from the driver (in Portrush, the Bushmills Open Topper bus stops at Dunluce Avenue, next to public WC, a 2-min walk from TI). For more info, call Translink (tel. 028/9066-6630, www.translink .co.uk).

By Bus Tour: If you're based in Belfast, you can visit sights on the Antrim Coast with a **McComb's** tour. Those based in Derry can get to the Giant's Causeway on a **Top Tours** tour.

By Car: Distances are short and parking is easy. Don't miss the treacherous-yet-scenic coastal route down to the Glens of Antrim.

By Taxi: Groups (up to four) go reasonably by taxi, which costs about £10 from Portrush to the Giant's Causeway. Try Andy Brown's Taxi (028/7082-2223), Hugh's Taxi (mobile 077-0298-6110), or North West Taxi (tel. 028/7082-4446).

Portrush

Homey Portrush used to be known as "the Brighton of the North." It first became a resort in the late 1800s as railroads expanded to offer the new middle class a weekend by the shore. Victorian society believed that swimming in salt water would cure many common ailments.

While it's seen its best days, Portrush retains the atmosphere and architecture of a genteel seaside resort. Its peninsula is filled with family-oriented amusements, fun eateries, and B&Bs. Summertime fun-seekers promenade along the tiny harbor and tumble down to the sandy beaches, which extend in sweeping white crescents on either side.

Superficially, Portrush has the appearance of any small British seaside resort, but its history and large population of young people (students from the University of Ulster at Coleraine) give the town a little more personality. Along with the usual arcade amusements, there are nightclubs, restaurants, summer theater (July–Aug) in the town hall, and convivial pubs that attract customers all the way from Belfast.

Orientation to Portrush

(area code: 028)

Portrush's pleasant and easily walkable town center features sea views in every direction. On one side are the harbor and most of the restaurants, and on the other are Victorian townhouses and vast, salty views. The tip of the peninsula is filled with tennis courts, lawn-bowling greens, putting greens, and a park.

The town is busy with students during the school year. July and August are beach-resort boom time. June and September are laid-back and lazy. Families pack Portrush on Saturdays, and revelers from Belfast crowd its hotels on Saturday nights.

Tourist Information

The TI, more generous and helpful than those in the Republic, is in the big, modern Dunluce Centre (July–Aug daily 9:00–19:00; April–June and Sept Mon–Fri 9:00–17:00, Sat–Sun 12:00–17:00; March and Oct Sat–Sun 12:00–17:00, closed Mon–Fri; closed Nov–Feb; tel. 028/7082-3333). Get the Collins Northern Ireland road map (£4), the free *Visitor Attractions* brochure, and a free Belfast map if you're Belfast-bound.

Arrival in Portrush

The train tracks stop at the base of the tiny peninsula that Portrush fills (no baggage storage at station). The TI is three long blocks from the train station (follow signs down Eglinton Street and turn left at the fire station). All listed B&Bs are within a 10-minute walk of the train station (see "Sleeping in Portrush"). The bus stop is two blocks from the train station.

Helpful Hints

Phone Tips: To call the Republic of Ireland from Northern Ireland, dial 00-353, then the area code without its initial 0, then the local number. To call Northern Ireland from the Republic of Ireland, dial 048, then the local eight-digit number.

Internet Access: Ground Espresso Bar has coin-op machines with fast connections (daily June–Aug 8:30–22:00, Sept–May 8:30–18:00, 52 Main Street, tel. 028/7082-5979).

Laundry: Viking Launderette charges £9/load for full service (Mon–Tue & Thu–Fri 9:00–17:30 except closed 13:00–14:00 for lunch, Sat 9:00–13:00, closed Sun and Wed, 68 Causeway Street, tel. 028/7082-2060).

Sights in Portrush

Barry's Old Time Amusement Arcade—This is a fine chance to see Northern Ireland at play (open weekends and summer only). Located just below the train station on the harbor, it's filled with candy floss (cotton candy) and little kids learning the art of one-armed bandits, 10p at a time. Get £1 worth of 10p coins from the machine and go wild, or brave the roller coaster and bumper cars (May–June Mon–Fri 10:00–18:00, Sat 12:30–22:30, Sun 12:30–21:30; July–mid-Sept daily 12:30–22:30; closed mid-Sept–April).

Portrush

1. Adelphi Guest House & Bistro
2. Beulah Guest House
3. Anvershiel B&B
4. Ardenlee B&B
5. Harbour Heights B&B
6. The Scullery Deli
7. Ground Espresso Bar & Internet Access
8. 55 North Rest. & Down Under Café
9. Harbour Road Eateries & Waterworld
10. Spring Hill Pub
11. Launderette

Pitch-and-Putt at the Royal Portrush Golf Course—Irish courses, like those in Scotland, are highly sought after for their lush but dry greens in glorious settings. Serious golfers can get a tee time at the Royal Portrush, occasional home of the Senior British Open (greens fees Mon–Fri-£125, Sat–Sun-£140). Those on a budget can play the adjacent, slightly shorter Valley Course (greens fees Mon–Fri-£35, Sat–Sun-£40). Meanwhile, rookies can get a wee dose of this wonderful golf setting at the neighboring Skerry 9 Hole Links pitch-and-putt range. You get two clubs and balls for £6, and they don't care if you go around twice (daily 8:30–19:00, 10-min walk from station, tel. 028/7082-2311).

Portrush Recreation Grounds—For some easygoing exercise right in town, this well-organized park offers lawn-bowling greens (£3.50/hr with gear), putting greens, tennis courts, a great kids' play park, and a snack bar. Tennis shoes, balls, and rackets can all be rented for a low price (mid-May–mid-Sept Mon–Sat 10:00–dusk, Sun 13:00–19:00, closed mid-Sept–mid-May, tel. 028/7082-4441).

More Fun—Consider **Dunluce Centre** (kid-oriented fun zone, in same building with TI) and **Waterworld** (£4.50, pool, waterslides, bowling; June–Aug daily 10:00–19:00; closed Sept–May; wedged between the Harbour Bistro and Ramore Wine Bar, tel. 028/7082-2001).

Sleeping in Portrush

Portrush has a range of hotels from decent to ritzy. Some B&Bs can be well-worn. August and Saturday nights can be tight. Otherwise, it's a "you take half a loaf when you can get it" town. Rates vary with the view and season—probe for softness. Many listings face the sea, though sea views are worth paying for only if you get a bay window. Ask for a big room (some doubles can be very small; twins are bigger). Lounges are invariably grand and have bay-window views. All places listed have lots of stairs, but most are perfectly central and within a few minutes' walk of the train station. Parking is easy.

$$$ Adelphi Guest House is a breath of fresh air, with 25 tastefully furnished modern rooms, friendly staff, and a hearty bistro downstairs (Sb-£55–105, Db-£65–115, Tb-£75–125, Qb-£105–155, 67–71 Main Street, Wi-Fi, tel. 028/7082-5544, www.adelphiportrush.com, stay@adelphiportrush.com).

$$ Beulah Guest House is an old-fashioned, good-value place. It's centrally located and run by cheerful Rachel Anderson, with 11 prim and smoke-free rooms (Ss-£32.50, Sb-£45–60, Db-£60–75, Tb-£85–95, parking, 16 Causeway Street, tel. 028/7082-2413, www.beulahguesthouse.com, stay@beulahguesthouse.com).

PORTRUSH

Sleep Code

(£1 = about $1.60, country code: 44, area code: 028)
To call Portrush from the Republic of Ireland, dial 048 before the local 8-digit number.

S = Single, **D** = Double/Twin, **T** = Triple, **Q** = Quad, **b** = bathroom, **s** = shower only. Breakfast is included and credit cards are accepted unless otherwise noted.

To help you easily sort through these listings, I've divided the rooms into two categories, based on the price for a standard double room with bath:

$$$ Higher Priced—Most rooms £80 or more.
 $$ Moderately Priced—Most rooms between £50–80.

$$ Anvershiel B&B, with six non-smoking rooms, is a five-minute walk south of the train station. Jovial Victor Bow, who runs the show with his wife Erna, is in the know about local golf (Sb-£45, Db-£65, Tb-£95, Qb-£125; 10 percent discount on Db with cash and 2-night stay Sept–June—not valid July–Aug; Wi-Fi, parking, 16 Coleraine Road, tel. 028/7082-3861, www.anvershiel .com, enquiries@anvershiel.com).

$$ Ardenlee B&B offers six smartly refurbished rooms, some with fine views of the ocean (Sb-£35–50, Db-£60–90, Tb-£100, 19 Kerr Street, tel. 028/7082-2639, mobile 077-1892-8756, russell .rafferty@btconnect.com).

$$ Harbour Heights B&B rents nine homey rooms, each named after a different town in County Antrim. It has an inviting guest lounge, DVD players, and a small DVD library (Sb-£40, Db-£70–80, sea view Db-£90, family rooms, Wi-Fi, 17 Kerr Street, tel. 028/7082-2765, mobile 078-9586-6534, fax 028/7082-2653, www.harbourheightsportrush.com, info@harbourheightsportrush .com, Sam and Tim Swart).

Eating in Portrush

Being a get-away-from-Belfast town and close to a university town (Coleraine), Portrush has more than enough chips joints. Eglinton Street is lined with cheap and cheery eateries.

Lunch Spots

The Scullery makes sandwiches and healthy wraps to take away and enjoy by the beach—or on an Antrim Coast picnic (daily 8:30–17:00, close to the train station at 4 Eglinton Lane, tel. 028/7082-1000).

Ground Espresso Bar makes fresh £4 sandwiches or paninis, soup, and excellent coffee (daily June–Aug 9:00–22:00, Sept–May 9:00–17:00, Main Street, tel. 028/7082-5979). They also offer coin-op Internet access (described earlier under "Helpful Hints").

55 Down Under Café serves basic sandwiches with a great patio view (Mon–Tue 9:00–17:00, Wed–Sun 9:00–21:00, shorter hours off-season, 1 Causeway Street, underneath fancier 55 North restaurant run by same owners and listed below, tel. 028/7082-2811).

Fine Dining

55 North (named for the local latitude) has the best sea views in town, with windows on all sides. The classy pasta-and-fish plates are a joy (£9–17 plates, daily 12:30–14:00 & 17:00–21:00 except closed Mon Sept–June, 1 Causeway Street, tel. 028/7082-2811).

Adelphi Bistro is a good bet for its relaxed family-friendly atmosphere and hearty meals (daily 12:00–15:00 & 17:00–21:00, 67–71 Main Street, tel. 028/7082-5544).

Harbour Road Eateries: The following four restaurants are located within 50 yards of each other (all under the same owner-ship and overlooking the harbor on Harbour Road), offering some of the best food values in town.

Ramore Wine Bar—salty, modern, and much-loved—bursts with happy eaters. They're enjoying the most inviting menu that I've seen in Ireland, featuring huge meals ranging from steaks to vegetarian food. Share a piece of the decadent banoffee (banana toffee) pie with a friend (£9–15 plates, daily 12:15–14:15 & 17:00–21:30, closes Sun at 21:00, tel. 028/7082-4313).

Downstairs, sharing the same building as the Ramore Wine Bar, is the energetic **Coast Italiano,** with (no surprise) great Italian dishes. Come early for a table or sit at the bar (Mon–Fri 17:00–22:00, Sat 16:30–22:00, Sun 15:00–21:00, Sept–June closed Mon–Tue, tel. 028/7082-3311).

The Harbour Bistro offers a more subdued, darker bistro ambience than the previous eateries, with meals for a few pounds more (£9–16 dinners, daily 17:00–21:30, tel. 028/7082-2430).

Ramore Oriental sits at the high end of the bunch, farthest from the water, and serves the best Asian cuisine in town (£10–15 dinners, Wed–Sat 18:30–22:30, Sun 18:00–21:30, closed Mon–Tue, tel. 028/7082-4313).

Pubs

The **Harbour Bar** (next to the Harbour Bistro) has an old-fashioned pub downstairs and a plush, overstuffed, dark lounge upstairs. Or try the **Spring Hill Pub** (Causeway Street), with a friendly vibe and occasional music session nights.

Portrush Connections

Consider a £15 "Day Tracker" ticket, good for all-day train and bus use in Northern Ireland year-round. Useful updated schedules and prices for both trains and buses in Northern Ireland can be obtained from Translink (tel. 028/9066-6630, www.translink.co.uk).

From Portrush by Train to: Coleraine (hourly, 12 min, sparse on Sun morning), **Belfast** (11/day Mon–Sat, 5/day Sun, 2 hrs, transfer in Coleraine), **Dublin** (7/day Mon–Sat, 2/day Sun, 5 hrs, transfer in Coleraine or Belfast).

By Bus to: Belfast (12/day, 2 hrs; scenic coastal route, 2.5 hrs), **Dublin** (4/day, 5.5 hrs).

Antrim Coast

The craggy 20-mile stretch of the Antrim Coast, extending eastward from Portrush to Ballycastle, rates second only to the tip of the Dingle Peninsula as the prettiest chunk of coastal Ireland. From your base in Portrush, you have a varied grab bag of sightseeing choices: the Giant's Causeway, Old Bushmills Distillery, Dunluce Castle, Carrick-a-Rede Rope Bridge, and Rathlin Island.

It's easy to weave these sites together by car, but connections are patchy by public transportation. Bus service is viable only in summer, and taxi fares are most reasonable for the sites closest to Portrush (Dunluce Castle and the Old Bushmills Distillery). For more on your transportation options, see "Getting Around the Antrim Coast," earlier.

Planning Your Time

With a car, you can do the Giant's Causeway, Old Bushmills Distillery, Dunluce Castle, and Carrick-a-Rede Rope Bridge in one busy day. Call ahead to reserve the Old Bushmills Distillery tour, and get an early start. Arrive at the Giant's Causeway by 9:00 when crowds are sparse. Park your car in the causeway lot and pay as you exit (after the center opens). Although the Causeway's visitors center doesn't open (and the shuttle bus doesn't run) until 10:00, the trails are free and always open. Spend 90 minutes scrambling over Ireland's most unique alligator-skin geology.

Then catch a late-morning tour of the Old Bushmills Distillery, a 400-year-old whiskey distillery. Grab a cheap lunch in the hospitality room afterwards. A 20-minute drive east brings you to Carrick-a-Rede, where you can enjoy a scenic cliff-top trail hike all the way to the lofty rope bridge (one hour round-trip, 1.5 hours if you cross the rope bridge and explore the sea stack). Hop in your car and double back west all the way to dramatically cliff-perched Dunluce Castle for a late afternoon tour. From here, you're only a five-minute drive away from Portrush.

Those with extra time, a car, and a hankering to seek out dramatic coastal cliff scenery may want to spend a half-day boating out to Rathlin Island, Northern Ireland's only inhabited island.

▲Dunluce Castle

These romantic ruins, perched dramatically on the edge of a rocky headland, are testimony to this region's turbulent past. During

the Middle Ages, the castle resisted several sieges. But on a stormy night in 1639, dinner was interrupted as half of the kitchen fell into the sea and took the servants with it. That was the last straw for the lady of the castle. The countess of Antrim packed up and moved inland, and the castle "began its slow submission to the forces of nature." While it's one of the largest castles in Northern Ireland and is beautifully situated, there's precious little left to see among its broken walls.

The 16th-century expansion of the castle was financed by the salvaging of a shipwreck. In 1588, the Spanish Armada's *Girona* sank on her way home after the aborted mission against England, laden with sailors and the valuables of three abandoned sister ships. More than 1,300 drowned, and only 5 survivors washed ashore. The shipwreck was excavated in 1967, and a bounty of golden odds and silver ends wound up in Belfast's Ulster Museum (closed for renovation until early 2010).

Castle admission includes an impromptu guided tour of the ruins. The tour is interesting for its effort to defend the notion of "Ulster, a place apart—facing Scotland, cut off from the rest of Ireland by dense forests and mountains..." Before you leave, poke your head into the building opposite the gift shop and check out the large castle model, which shows the joint in its fully roofed heyday (£2, daily April–Sept 10:00–18:00, off-season 10:00–16:30, last entry 30 min before closing, tel. 028/2073-1938).

▲▲Giant's Causeway

This four-mile-long stretch of coastline, a World Heritage Site, is famous for its bizarre basalt columns. The shore is covered with largely hexagonal pillars that stick up at various heights. It's

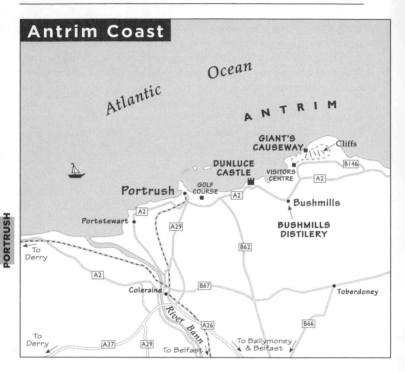

Antrim Coast

Atlantic Ocean

ANTRIM

GIANT'S
CAUSEWAY Cliffs

DUNLUCE
CASTLE B146

VISITORS
CENTRE A2

Portrush GOLF
COURSE A2

• Bushmills

A2 BUSHMILLS
DISTILERY

Portstewart •

A29

To B62
Derry

A2

Coleraine B67 Toberdoney •

River Bann

To A26 B66
Derry

A37 A29 To Ballymoney
To Belfast & Belfast

as if the earth were offering God his choice of 37,000 six-sided cigarettes.

Geologists claim the Giant's Causeway was formed by volcanic eruptions more than 60 million years ago. As the surface of the lava flow quickly cooled, it contracted and cracked into hexagonal columns. As the rock (which looked like alligator skin) later settled and eroded, the columns broke off into many stair-like steps.

Of course, in actuality, the Giant's Causeway was made by a giant Ulster warrior named Finn MacCool who wanted to reach his love on the Scottish island of Staffa. Way back then, the causeway stretched to Scotland, connecting the two lands. Today, while the foundation has settled, the formation still extends undersea to Staffa, just off the Scottish coast. Finn's causeway was ruined (into today's "remnant of chaos") by a rival giant. As the rival fled from ferocious Finn back to his Scottish homeland, he ripped up the causeway so Finn couldn't chase him.

For cute variations on the Finn story, as well as details on the ridiculous theories of modern geologists, start your visit in

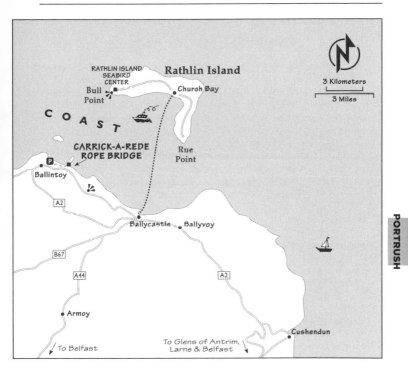

RATHLIN ISLAND
SEABIRD
CENTER

Rathlin Island

Bull Point

Church Bay

C O A S T

3 Kilometers

3 Miles

**CARRICK-A-REDE
ROPE BRIDGE**

Rue
Point

P

Ballintoy

A2

Ballycastle   Ballyvoy

B67

A44

A2

Armoy

Cushendun

To Belfast

To Glens of Antrim,
Larne & Belfast

the visitors center (free entry but £6 to park, daily 10:00–17:00, July–Aug until 18:00, tel. 028/2073-1855, www.nationaltrust.org .uk). A 12-minute video gives a worthwhile history of the Giant's Causeway, with a regional overview (£1, 4/hr). A gift shop and cafeteria are standing by.

A minibus (4/hr, £1 each way) zips tired tourists a half-mile directly from the visitors center to the Giant's Causeway, the highlight of the entire coast.

For a better dose of the causeway, consider this plan: Follow the high cliff-top trail uphill from the visitors center 10 minutes to a great precipice viewpoint, then walk 15 minutes farther to reach the Shepherd's Stairway. Zigzag down the stairs and switchbacks to the coast; at the T junction, go 100 yards right to the towering pipes of "the Organ." Then retrace your steps and continue left down to the tidal zone, where the "Giant's Boot" (on the right) provides some photo fun. Another 100 yards farther you'll find the dramatic point where the stairs step into the sea. Just beyond that, at the asphalt turnaround, you'll see the bus stop for a lift back to the visitors center. You could also walk the entire five-mile-long Giant's Causeway. The 75p hiking guide points out the highlights named by 18th-century guides (Camel's Back, Giant's Eye, and so on). The causeway itself is free and always open.

The Scottish Connection

The Romans called the Irish the "Scoti" (meaning pirates). When the Scoti crossed the narrow Irish Sea and invaded the land of the Picts 1,500 years ago, that region became known as Scotland. Ireland and Scotland were never conquered by the Romans, and they retained similar clannish Celtic traits. Both share the same Gaelic branch of the linguistic tree.

On clear summer days from Carrick-a-Rede, the island of Mull in Scotland—only 17 miles away—is visible. Much closer on the horizon is the boomerang-shaped Rathlin Island, part of Northern Ireland. Rathlin is where Scottish leader Robert the Bruce (a compatriot of William "Braveheart" Wallace) retreated in 1307 after defeat at the hands of the English. Legend has it that he hid in a cave on the island, where he observed a spider patiently rebuilding its web each time a breeze knocked it down. Inspired by the spider's perseverance, Robert gathered his Scottish forces once more and finally defeated the English at the decisive battle of Bannockburn.

Flush with confidence from his victory, Robert the Bruce decided to open up a second front against the English...in Ireland. In 1315, he sent his brother Edward over to enlist their Celtic Irish

Tourist Train: In summer, a quaint, narrow-gauge steam locomotive connects the causeway to the town of Bushmills with a two-mile, 15-minute journey (£5.25 one-way, £6.75 round-trip, daily July–Aug, only on weekends June and Sept, tel. 028/2073-2844, www.freewebs.com/giantscausewayrailway). The train runs hourly, departing the causeway's station at the top of the hour (11:00–17:00), and leaving Bushmills station on the half-hour (11:30–17:30, on Ballaghmore Road, a 15-min walk from distillery).

▲▲Old Bushmills Distillery

Bushmills claims to be the world's oldest distillery. Though King James I (of Bible fame) only granted its license to distill "Aqua Vitae" in 1608, whiskey has been made here since the 13th century. Distillery tours waft you through the process, making it clear that Irish whiskey is triple distilled—and therefore smoother than Scotch whisky (distilled merely twice and minus the "e"). The 45-minute tour starts with the mash pit, which is filled with a porridge that eventually becomes whiskey. (The leftovers of that porridge are fed to the county's particularly happy cows.) You'll see thousands of oak

cousins in an effort to thwart the English. After securing Ireland, Edward hoped to move on and enlist the Welsh, thus cornering England with their pan-Celtic nation. But Edward's timing was bad—Ireland was in the midst of famine. His Scottish troops had to live off the land and began to take food and supplies from the starving Irish. He might also have been trying to destroy Ireland's crops to keep them from being used as a colonial "breadbasket" to feed English troops. The Scots quickly wore out their welcome, and Edward the Bruce was eventually killed in battle near Dundalk in 1318.

This was the first time in history that Ireland was used as a pawn by England's enemies. Ireland was seen as the English Achilles' heel by Spain and France, who later attempted Irish invasions. The English Tudor and Stuart royalty countered these threats in the 16th and 17th centuries by starting the "plantation" of loyal subjects in Ireland. The only successful long-term settlement by the English was here in Northern Ireland, which remains part of the United Kingdom today.

It's interesting to speculate how things would be different today if Ireland and Scotland had been permanently welded together as a nation 700 years ago. You'll notice the strong Scottish influence in this part of Ireland when you ask a local a question and he answers, "Aye, a wee bit." The Irish joke that the Scots are just Irish people who couldn't swim home.

casks—the kind used for Spanish sherry—filled with aging whiskey.

The finale, of course, is the opportunity for a sip in the 1608 Bar—the former malt barn. Everyone gets a single glass of his or her choice. Hot-drink enthusiasts might enjoy a cinnamon-and-cloves hot toddy.

To see the distillery at its lively best, visit when the 100 workers are staffing the machinery—Monday morning through Friday noon (weekend tours see a still still). Tours are limited to 35 people and book up. In summer, call and put in your name to get a tour time before you arrive (£6; April–Oct tours on the half-hour Mon–Sat from 9:30, Sun from 12:00, last tour at 16:00; Nov–March tours Mon–Sat at 10:00, 11:00, 12:00, 13:30, 14:30, and 15:30, Sun from 12:00; tel. 028/2073-1521, www.bushmills.com). You can get a decent lunch in the tasting room after your tour. Look for the distillery sign a quarter mile from Bushmills town center.

▲▲Carrick-a-Rede Rope Bridge

For 200 years, fishermen have hung a narrow, 90-foot-high bridge (planks strung between wires) across a 65-foot-wide chasm

PORTRUSH

between the mainland and a tiny island. Today, the bridge (while not the original version) still gives access to the salmon nets that are set during the summer months to catch the fish turning the coast's corner. (The complicated system is described at the gateway.) A pleasant, 30-minute one-mile walk from the parking lot takes you to the rope bridge. Cross to the island for fine views and great seabird-watching, especially during nesting season (£4 trail and bridge fee, pay at hut beside parking lot, coffee shop and WCs near parking lot, March–Oct daily 10:00–18:00, July–Aug until 19:00, closed Nov–Feb, tel. 028/2076-9839, www.nationaltrust.org.uk).

If you have a car and a picnic lunch, don't miss the terrific coastal viewpoint rest area one mile steeply uphill and east of Carrick-a-Rede (on B-15 road to Ballycastle). This grassy area offers one of the best picnic views in Northern Ireland (picnic tables but no WCs). Feast on bird's-eye views of the rope bridge, nearby Rathlin Island (described next), and the not-so-distant Island of Mull in Scotland.

Rathlin Island

The only inhabited island off the coast of Northern Ireland, Rathlin is a quiet haven for hikers, bird-watchers, and seal spotters. The Rathlin Island ferry departs from Ballycastle, just east of Carrick-a-Rede. It does nine crossings per day in summer. Five are fast 20-minute trips on passenger boats, and four are slower 45-minute trips on car ferries (£10.60 round-trip per passenger on either type of boat, reserve ahead, tel. 028/2076-9299, www.rathlinballycastleferry.com).

Travelers with rental cars will have no problem reaching Ballycastle. A taxi from Portrush to Ballycastle runs £20 one-way. Bus service from Portrush to Ballycastle is spotty (check with the TI in Portrush, or contact Translink—tel. 028/9066-6630, www.translink.co.uk).

Rathlin Island is "L"-shaped and less than seven miles from end to end. Its population of 75 islanders cluster around the ferry dock at Church Bay. Here you'll find the Rathlin Manor House, offering the island's most convenient lodging, a restaurant, and a pub (tel. 028/2076-3964, www.rathlinmanorhouse.co.uk). The **Rathlin Boathouse Visitor Centre** operates as the island's TI (May–Aug daily 10:30–13:30 & 14:00–16:00, on the bay 100 yards east of the ferry dock, tel. 028/2076-2225).

In summer, the Puffin shuttle bus (£5 round-trip, seats 25) meets arriving ferries and drives visitors to the **Rathlin Island Seabird Centre** at the west end of the island. Here a lighthouse extends down the cliff with its beacon at the bottom. It's upside down because the coast guard wants the light visible only from a certain distance out to sea. The bird observation terrace at the Centre (next to the lighthouse) overlooks one of the most dramatic coastal views in Ireland—a sheer drop of over 300 feet to craggy sea stacks just off-shore, draped in thousands of sea birds. Photographers will want to bring their most-powerful zoom lens.

For such a snoozy island, Rathlin has seen its fair share of history. Flint axe-heads were quarried here in Neolithic times. The island was one of the first in Ireland to be raided by Vikings in 795. Robert the Bruce hid out from English pursuers on Rathlin in the early 1300s (see "The Scottish Connection" sidebar). In the late 1500s, local warlord Sorely Boy MacDonnell stashed his extended family on Rathlin and waited on the mainland at Dunluce Castle to face his English enemies...only to watch in horror as they headed for the island instead to massacre his loved ones. And in 1917, a WWI U-boat sank the British cruiser HMS *Drake* in Church Bay. (The wreck is now a popular scuba-dive destination.)

▲Antrim Mountains and Glens

Not particularly high (never more than 1,500 feet), the Antrim Mountains are cut by a series of large glens running northeast to the sea. Glenariff, with its waterfalls (especially the Mare's Tail), is the most beautiful of the nine glens. Travelers going by car can take a pleasant drive from Portrush to Belfast, sticking to the A-2 road that takes in parts of all of the Glens of Antrim. The two best stops en route are Cushendall (nice beach for a picnic) and the castle at Carrickfergus.

DERRY AND COUNTY DONEGAL

The town of Derry (or Londonderry to Unionists) is the mecca of Ulster Unionism. When Ireland was being divvied up, the River Foyle was the logical border between the North and the Republic. But, for sentimental and economic reasons, the North kept Derry, which is on the Republic's side of the river. Consequently, this predominantly Catholic city has been much contested throughout the Troubles.

Even its name is disputed. While most of its population and its city council call it "Derry," some maps, road signs, and train schedules in the UK use "Londonderry," the name on its 1662 royal charter and the one favored by Unionists.

Still, the conflict is only one dimension of Derry; this pivotal city has a more diverse history and a prettier setting than Belfast. Derry was a vibrant city back when Belfast was just a mudflat. And with a quarter of the population (84,000), Derry feels more manageable to visitors.

County Donegal, to the west of Derry, is about as far-flung as Ireland gets. A forgotten economic backwater (part of the Republic but riding piggyback on the North), it lacks blockbuster museums or sights. But a visit here is more about the journey, and adventurous drivers—a car is a must—will be rewarded with a time-capsule peek into old Irish ways and uncompromisingly beautiful scenery.

Planning Your Time

Travelers heading north from Westport or Galway should get an early start. Donegal town makes a good lunch stop, with lots of choices surrounding its triangular town square, and then it's on to

Derry, where you can spend a couple of hours seeing the essentials. Visit the Tower Museum and catch some views from the town wall before continuing on to Portrush for the night.

With more time, spend a night in Derry, so you can see the powerful Bogside murals and take a walking tour around the town walls—you'll appreciate this underrated city. With two nights in Derry, consider crossing the border into the Republic for a scenic driving loop through part of remote County Donegal.

Derry

No city in Ireland connects the kaleidoscope of historical dots more colorfully than Derry. From a leafy monastic hamlet to a Viking-pillaged port, from a cannonball-battered siege survivor to an Industrial Revolution sweatshop, from an essential WWII naval base to a wrenching flashpoint of sectarian Troubles...Derry has seen it all.

Lately there have been some refreshing changes. The manned British Army surveillance towers were taken down in 2006, and the British troops themselves finally departed in mid-2007, after 38 years in Northern Ireland. Today, you can feel comfortable wandering the streets and enjoying this unique Irish city.

Orientation to Derry

(area code: 028)
The River Foyle flows north, slicing Derry into eastern and western chunks. The old town walls and worthwhile sights are all on the west side. Waterloo Place and the adjacent Guildhall Square, just outside the north corner of the old city walls, are the pedestrian hubs of city activity. The Strand Road area extending north from Waterloo Place makes a comfortable home base, with the majority of lodging and restaurant suggestions within a block or two on either side. The Diamond and its War Memorial statue mark the heart of the old city within the walls.

Tourist Information
The TI sits on the riverfront and has a room-finding service, books bus and walking tours (see "Tours in Derry"), and gives out free city maps (July–Sept Mon–Fri 9:00–19:00, Sat 10:00–18:00, Sun 10:00–17:00; Oct–June Mon–Fri 9:00–17:00, Sat 10:00–17:00, closed Sun; 44 Foyle Street, tel. 028/7126-7284, www.derry visitor.com).

Arrival in Derry

Next to the river on the east side of town, Derry's little end-of-the-line train station (no storage lockers) has service to Portrush, Belfast, and Dublin. Free shuttle buses to Ulsterbus station (which is on the west side of town) await each arriving train. Otherwise, it's a 15-minute walk across Craigavon Bridge to the TI, or a £4 taxi ride to Guildhall Square. The same free shuttle service leaves Ulsterbus station 15 minutes before each departing train. The Ulsterbus station is a couple minutes' walk south of Guildhall Square.

Derry is compact enough to see on foot; drivers stopping for a few hours can park at the Foyleside parking garage across from the TI (£0.80/hr, £2.20/4 hrs, Mon–Tue 8:00–19:00, Wed–Fri 8:00–22:00, Sat 8:00–20:00, Sun 12:00–19:00, tel. 028/7137-7575). Drivers staying overnight can ask about parking at their B&B or try the Quayside parking garage behind the Travelodge (£0.80/hr, £3/5 hours, Mon–Thu 7:30–21:00, Fri–Sat open 24 hours, Sun 12:30–18:00).

Helpful Hints

Phone Tips: To call the Republic of Ireland from Northern Ireland, dial 00-353, then the area code without its initial 0, then the local number. To call Northern Ireland from the Republic of Ireland, dial 048, then the local eight-digit number.

Money: Northern Bank is on Guildhall Square and the **Bank of Ireland** is on Strand Road (both open Mon–Fri 9:30–16:30, Sat 9:30–12:30, closed Sun).

Internet Access: Located inside the walls, **Claudes Café** is just north of the Diamond on Shipquay Street (£3/30 min, daily 9:00–17:30, tel. 028/7127-9379).

Post Office: The main post office is just off Waterloo Place (Mon–Fri 9:00–17:30, Sat 9:00–12:30, closed Sun, Custom House Street).

Laundry: Smooth Operators can do a load of laundry for £8.50 (drop off in morning to pick up later that day, Mon–Fri 8:30–18:00, Sat 8:30–17:30, closed Sun, 8 Sackville Street, tel. 028/7136-0529).

Taxi: Try **Derry Taxis** (tel. 028/7126-0247) or **Foyle Delta Cabs** (tel. 028/7127-9999).

Tours in Derry

Walking Tours—Martin McCrossan and his staff lead insightful 60-minute tours of the city, departing from 11 Carlisle Road just below Ferryquay Gate (£4; daily at 10:00, 12:00, and 14:00; call to confirm schedule, also offers private tours, tel. 028/7127-1996, mobile 077-1293-7997, www.irishtourguides.com).

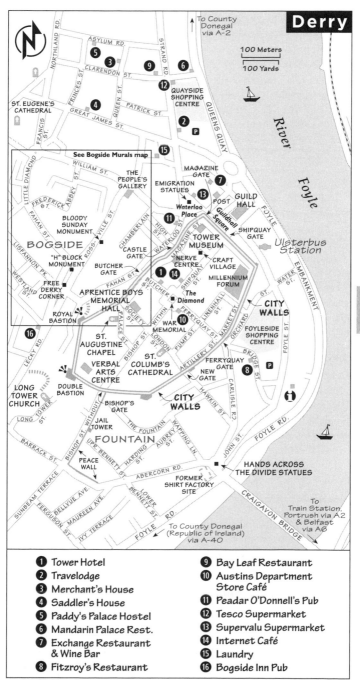

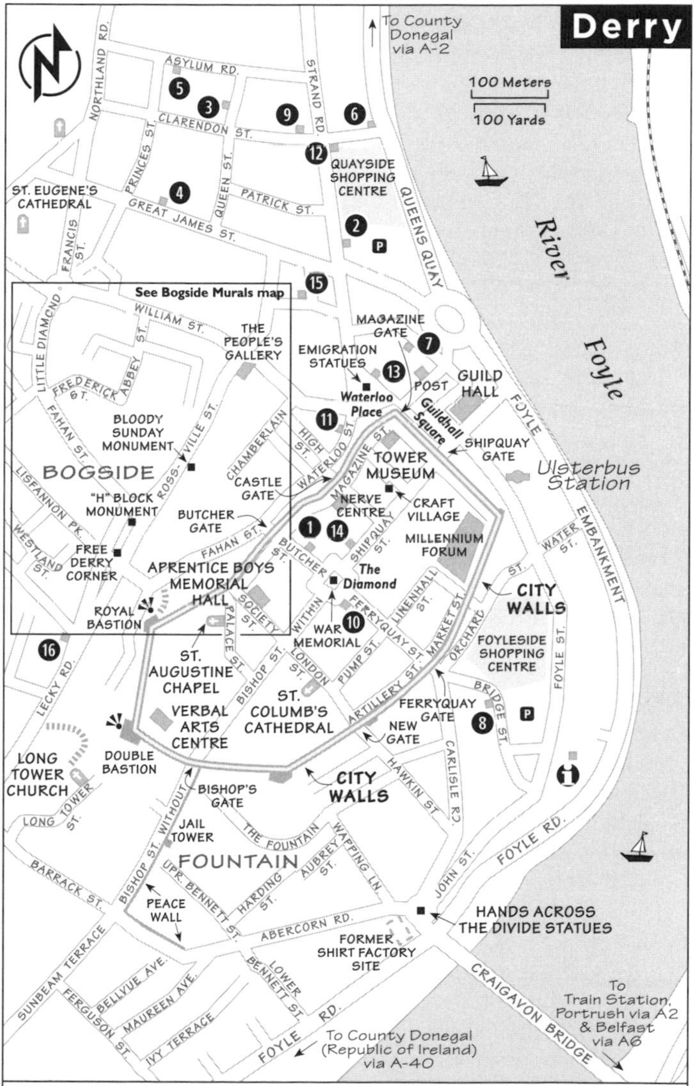
Derry
To County Donegal via A-2
100 Meters
100 Yards
River Foyle
Asylum Rd.
Northland Rd.
Clarendon St.
Strand Rd.
Princes St.
Queen St.
Patrick St.
Great James St.
St. Eugene's Cathedral
Francis St.
Quayside Shopping Centre
Queens Quay
See Bogside Murals map
William St.
Little Diamond
Frederick St.
Abbey St.
The People's Gallery
Magazine Gate
Emigration Statues
Waterloo Place
Post
Guild Hall
Guildhall Square
Foyle
Bloody Sunday Monument
Rossville St.
Fahan St.
Bogside
Chamberlain
Castle Gate
High St.
Waterloo St.
Magazine St.
Tower Museum
Shipquay Gate
Ulsterbus Station
Lisfannon Pk.
"H" Block Monument
Butcher Gate
Nerve Centre
Craft Village
Millennium Forum
Water St.
Embankment
Westland St.
Free Derry Corner
Aprentice Boys Memorial Hall
Butcher St.
Shipquay St.
The Diamond
Linenhall St.
City Walls
Royal Bastion
Society St.
Palace St.
Withing
War Memorial
Ferryquay St.
Market St.
Orchard St.
Foyleside Shopping Centre
Foyle St.
St. Augustine Chapel
Lecky Rd.
Bishop St.
London St.
Pump St.
St. Columb's Cathedral
Artillery St.
Ferryquay Gate
Bridge St.
Verbal Arts Centre
New Gate
Carlisle Rd.
Long Tower Church
Double Bastion
Long Tower St.
Bishop's Gate
City Walls
Hawkin St.
Jail Tower
The Fountain
Wapping Ln.
Fountain
Bishop St. Without
Barrack St.
Upr. Bennett St.
Harding St.
Aubrey St.
John St.
Foyle Rd.
Peace Wall
Hands Across the Divide Statues
Abercorn Rd.
Former Shirt Factory Site
Sunbeam Terrace
Bellvue Ave.
Ferguson St.
Maureen Ave.
Ivy Terrace
Lower Bennett St.
Foyle Rd.
To County Donegal (Republic of Ireland) via A-40
Craigavon Bridge
To Train Station, Portrush via A2 & Belfast via A6

1. Tower Hotel
2. Travelodge
3. Merchant's House
4. Saddler's House
5. Paddy's Palace Hostel
6. Mandarin Palace Rest.
7. Exchange Restaurant & Wine Bar
8. Fitzroy's Restaurant
9. Bay Leaf Restaurant
10. Austins Department Store Café
11. Peadar O'Donnell's Pub
12. Tesco Supermarket
13. Supervalu Supermarket
14. Internet Café
15. Laundry
16. Bogside Inn Pub

Stephen McPhilemy leads private tours of his hometown, Belfast, and the North Coast—when he's not on the road guiding Rick Steves tours several months a year (tel. 028/7130-9051, mobile 078-0101-1027, www.irishexperience.ie, steve@irish experience.ie). Stephen also runs the Paddy's Palace Hostel (listed under "Sleeping in Derry").

The **Bogside Artists** explain the impassioned inspiration behind their famous murals on walks departing from their studio, The People's Gallery, at the corner of Rossville and William streets (£4; daily at 11:00, 14:00, and 16:00; call to confirm schedule, tel. 028/7137-3842, Republic tel. 00353-74-9108-9997, www .bogsideartists.com).

Free Derry Tours depart daily at 10:00 and 14:00 from the Museum of Free Derry. Tours focus on the surrounding Bogside neighborhood's history as the flashpoint that ignited the modern Troubles (£6, tel. 028/7126-2812, mobile 077-9328-5972, www .freederry.net, freederrytours@gmail.com).

Bus Tours—**Top Tours'** double-decker buses are a good option on a rainy day. You'll be driven around the city in a 60-minute loop that covers both sides of the river, including Guild Hall, the old city walls, political wall murals (Nationalist as well as Unionist), cathedrals, and former shirt factories. Your ticket is good for one lap around the loop, and you stay on the bus for the duration (£8, pay driver, April–Sept daily on the hour 10:00–16:00, departs from in front of TI and beside the Guild Hall, www.toptoursireland.com).

Top Tours also offers trips from Derry to the Giant's Causeway and Carrick-a-Rede Rope Bridge in County Antrim (£20, runs daily May–Sept, depart TI at 11:00, return at 18:00, mobile 077-6318-1239).

All of their tours can be booked through the Derry TI.

Self-Guided Walks

Though calm today, Derry is marked by years of tumultuous conflict. These two walks (each taking less than an hour) will increase your understanding of the town's history. The first walk, starting on the old city walls and ending at the Anglican Cathedral, focuses on Derry's early days. The second walking tour helps you easily find the city's compelling murals, which document the time of the Troubles. These tours can be done separately or linked, depending on your time.

Walk the Walls

Squatting determinedly in the city center, the old city walls of Derry (built 1613–1618 and still intact, except for wider gates to handle modern vehicles) hold an almost mythic place in Irish history.

It was here in 1688 that a group of brave apprentice boys, many of whom had been shipped to Derry as orphans after the great fire of London in 1666, took their stand. They slammed the city gates shut in the face of the approaching Catholic forces of deposed King James II. With this act, the boys galvanized the city's indecisive Protestant defenders inside the walls.

Months of negotiations and a grinding 105-day siege followed, during which a third of the 20,000 refugees and defenders crammed into the city perished.

The siege was finally broken in 1689, when supply ships broke through a boom stretched across the River Foyle. The sacrifice and defiant survival of the city turned the tide in favor of newly crowned Protestant King William of Orange, who arrived in Ireland soon after and defeated James at the pivotal Battle of the Boyne.

To fully appreciate the walls, take a walk on top of them (free and open from dawn to dusk). Almost 20 feet high and at least as thick, the walls form a mile-long oval loop that you can cover in less than an hour. But the most interesting section is the half-circuit facing away from the river, starting at Magazine Gate (stairs face the Tower Museum Derry inside the walls) and finishing at Bishop's Gate.

From Magazine Gate, walk the wall as it heads uphill, snaking along the earth's contours like a mini–Great Wall of China. In the row of buildings on the left (just before crossing over Castle Gate), you'll see an arch entry into the **Craft Village,** an alley lined with a cluster of cute shops that showcase the recent economic rejuvenation of Derry (Mon–Sat 9:30–17:30, closed Sun).

• *After crossing over Butcher Gate, stop at the corner of Society Street (on the left) to view the...*

Apprentice Boys Memorial Hall: Built in 1873, it houses the private lodge and meeting rooms of an all-male Protestant organization. The group is dedicated to the memory of the original 13 apprentice boys who saved the day during the 1688 siege. Each year, on the Saturday closest to the August 12 anniversary date, the modern-day Apprentice Boys Society celebrates the end of the siege with a controversial march atop the walls. These walls are considered sacred ground for devout Unionists, who claim that many who died during the famous siege were buried within the battered walls because of lack of space.

Next, you'll pass a large, square pedestal on the right atop Royal Bastion. It once supported a column in honor of Governor

DERRY

George Walker, the commander of the defenders during the famous siege. In 1973, the IRA blew up the column, which had 105 steps to the top (one for each day of the siege). The governor's statue survived the blast and can be seen behind the Apprentice Boys Hall, down Society Street and behind a protective fence.

• *Opposite the empty pedestal is the small Anglican...*

St. Augustine Chapel: Set in a pretty graveyard, it's where some believe the original sixth-century monastery of St. Columba (St. Colmcille in Irish) stood. In Victorian times, this stretch of the walls was a fashionable promenade walk.

As you walk, you'll pass a wall (on the left)—all that's left of a British Army **surveillance tower** that stood here until 2006. Soldiers built it here for its bird's-eye view of the once-turbulent Catholic Bogside district below. The tower's dismantlement—as well as the removal of most of the British Army from Northern Ireland—is another positive sign in cautiously optimistic Derry. The walls of this former army base now contain a parking lot.

Stop at the Double Bastion **fortified platform** that occupies this corner of the city walls. The old cannon is nicknamed "Roaring Meg" for the fury of its firing during the siege.

From here, you can see across the Bogside to the not-so-far-away hills of County Donegal in the Republic. Derry was once an island, but as the River Foyle gradually changed its course, the area you see below the wall began to drain. Over time, and especially after the Great Potato Famine (1845–1849), Catholic peasants from rural Donegal began to move into Derry to find work during the Industrial Revolution. They settled on this least desirable land...on the soggy, bog side of the city.

Directly below and to the right are Free Derry Corner and Rossville Street, where the tragic events of Bloody Sunday took place in 1972 (described further in "Bogside Murals Walk," next page). Down on the left is the 18th-century Long Tower Catholic church, named after the monk-built round tower that once stood in the area.

• *Head to the grand brick building behind you.*

The Verbal Arts Centre: A former Presbyterian school, this center promotes the development of local literary arts in the form of poetry, drama, writing, and storytelling. Drop in for a cup of coffee in their coffeehouse and see what performances might be on during your visit (Mon–Thu 9:00–17:30, Fri 9:00–16:00, closed Sat–Sun, tel. 028/7126-6946, www.verbalartscentre.co.uk).

Continuing another 50 yards, go left around the corner and you'll reach Bishop's Gate, from which you can look up Bishop Street Within (inside the walls); this was the site of another British Army surveillance tower, placed just inside the town walls, which overlooked the neighborhood until 2006. Now look in the

other direction to see Bishop Street Without (outside the walls). You'll spot a modern wall topped by a high mesh fence; it runs along the left side of Bishop Street Without. This is a **peace wall**—built to ensure the security of the Protestant enclave living behind it—in Derry's Fountain neighborhood. When the Troubles reignited more than 40 years ago, 20,000 Protestants lived on this side of the river. Sadly, this small housing development of 1,000 people is all that remains of that proud community today. The rest have chosen to move across the river to the mostly Protestant Waterside district. The stone tower halfway down the peace wall was part of the old jail that briefly held doomed rebel Wolfe Tone after the 1798 revolt against the British.

• *From Bishop's Gate, those short on time can descend from the walls and walk 15 minutes directly back through the heart of the old city, along Bishop Street Within and Shipquay Street to Guildhall Square. With more time, consider visiting St. Columb's Cathedral, the Long Tower Church, and the murals of the Bogside.*

Bogside Murals Walk

The Catholic Bogside area was the tinderbox of the modern Troubles in Northern Ireland. A terrible confrontation more than 40 years ago sparked a sectarian inferno, and the ashes have not yet fully cooled. Today, the murals of the Bogside give visitors an accessible glimpse of this community's passionate perception of those events.

Inspired by civil rights marches in America in the mid-1960s, and the Prague Spring uprising and Paris student strikes of 1968, civil rights groups began to protest in Northern Ireland. Initially, their goals were to gain better housing, secure fair voting rights, and end employment discrimination for Catholics in the North. Tensions mounted, and clashes with the predominantly Protestant Royal Ulster Constabulary police force became frequent. Eventually, the British Army was called in to keep the peace. On January 30, 1972, a group protesting internment without trial held an illegal march through the Bogside neighborhood. They were fired upon by members of a British regiment, who claimed that snipers had fired on them first. The tragic result of the clash, now remembered as Bloody Sunday, caused the death of 14 civilians and led to a flood of fresh IRA volunteers.

The events are memorialized in 12 **murals** painted on the ends of residential flats along a 300-yard stretch of Rossville Street and

DERRY

Derry's History

Once an island in the River Foyle, Derry (from *daire,* Irish for "oak grove") was chosen by St. Colmcille (St. Columba in English) circa A.D. 546 for a monastic settlement. He later banished himself to the island of Iona in Scotland out of remorse for sparking a bloody battle over the rights to a holy manuscript that he had secretly copied.

A thousand years later, the English defeated the last Ulster-based Gaelic chieftains in the battle of Kinsale (1601). With victory at hand, the English took advantage of the power vacuum. They began the "plantation" of Ulster with loyal Protestant subjects imported from Scotland and England. The native Irish were displaced to less desirable rocky or boggy lands, sowing the seeds of resentment that fueled the modern-day Troubles.

A dozen wealthy London guilds (grocers, haberdashers, tailors, and others) took on Derry as an investment, and changed its name to "Londonderry." They built the last great walled city in Ireland to protect their investment from the surrounding—and hostile—Irish locals. The walls proved their worth in 1688–1689, when the town's Protestant defenders, loyal to King William of Orange, withstood a prolonged siege by the forces of Catholic King James II. "No surrender" is still a passionate rallying cry among Ulster Unionists determined to remain part of the United Kingdom.

The town became a major port of emigration to the New World in the early 1800s. Then, when the Industrial Revolution provided a steam-powered sewing factory, the city developed a thriving shirt-making industry. The factories here employed mostly Catholic women who had honed their skills in rural County Donegal. Although Belfast grew larger and wealthier, Unionists tightened their grip on "Londonderry" and the walls that they regarded with almost holy reverence. In 1921, they insisted that the city be included in Northern Ireland when the province was partitioned from the new Irish Free State (later to become the

Lecky Road, where the march took place. You can reach them from Waterloo Place via William Street, from the old city walls at Butcher Gate via the long set of stairs extending below Fahan Street on the grassy hillside, or by the stairs leading down from the Long Tower Church. These days, this neighborhood is gritty but quiet and safe.

Two brothers and their childhood friend became known as the Bogside Artists. They grew up in the Bogside and witnessed the tragic events that took place there, which led them to begin painting the murals in 1994. One of the brothers, Tom Kelly, gained a reputation as a "heritage mural" painter, specializing in scenes of life in the old days. In a surprising and hopeful development,

Republic of Ireland). A bit of gerrymandering (three lightly populated Unionist districts outvoted two densely populated Nationalist districts) ensured that the Protestant minority maintained control of the city, despite its Catholic majority.

Derry was a key escort base for US convoys headed for Britain during World War II, and 60 surviving German U-boats

were instructed to surrender here at the end of the war. After the war, poor Catholics—unable to find housing—took over the abandoned military barracks, with multiple families living in each dwelling. Only homeowners were allowed to vote, and the Unionist minority, which controlled city government, was not eager to build more

housing that would tip the voting balance away from them. Over the years, sectarian pressures gradually built—until they reached the boiling point. Then, the ugly events of Bloody Sunday on January 30, 1972, brought worldwide attention to the Troubles (see "Bogside Murals Walk," page 61).

Today, life has stabilized in Derry, and the population has increased by 25 percent in the last 30 years, to about 84,000. The modern Foyleside Shopping Centre, bankrolled by investors from Boston, opened in 1995. The 1998 Good Friday Peace Accord has provided two-steps-forward, one-step-back progress toward peace, and the British Army withdrew 90 percent of its troops in mid-2007. With a population that is 70 percent Catholic, the city has agreed to alternate Nationalist and Unionist mayors. There is a feeling of cautious optimism as Derry—the epicenter of bombs and bloody conflicts in the 1960s and 1970s—now boasts a history museum that airs all viewpoints.

DERRY

Kelly was invited into Derry's Protestant Fountain neighborhood to work with a youth club there on three proud heritage murals that were painted over paramilitary graffiti.

You can visit **The People's Gallery** (the Bogside Artists' studio) to gain an understanding of the inspiration that led to their memorable works. Ask to watch the illuminating 15-minute interview with the artists that aired on Irish TV (free entry, daily 10:00–18:00, corner of Rossville and William Streets, tel. 028/7137-3842, www.bogsideartists.com). Then take one of their walking tours (£4, described earlier under "Tours in Derry") to learn about the murals from the artists themselves. If they're unavailable, take the following walk.

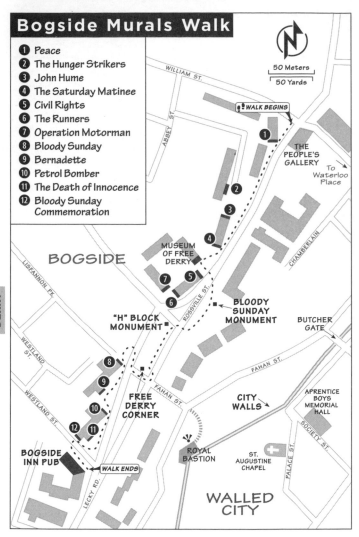

Bogside Murals Walk

1. Peace
2. The Hunger Strikers
3. John Hume
4. The Saturday Matinee
5. Civil Rights
6. The Runners
7. Operation Motorman
8. Bloody Sunday
9. Bernadette
10. Petrol Bomber
11. The Death of Innocence
12. Bloody Sunday Commemoration

50 Meters
50 Yards

WALK BEGINS

THE PEOPLE'S GALLERY

To Waterloo Place

WILLIAM ST.

ABBEY ST.

CHAMBERLAIN

BOGSIDE

LISFANNON PK.

MUSEUM OF FREE DERRY

BLOODY SUNDAY MONUMENT

BUTCHER GATE

"H" BLOCK MONUMENT

ROSSVILLE ST.

WESTLAND ST.

FAHAN ST.

CITY WALLS

APPRENTICE BOYS MEMORIAL HALL

FREE DERRY CORNER

SOCIETY ST.

PALACE ST.

BOGSIDE INN PUB

WALK ENDS

LECKY RD.

ROYAL BASTION

ST. AUGUSTINE CHAPEL

WALLED CITY

DERRY

The Bogside murals face different directions (and some are partially hidden by buildings), so they're not all visible from a single viewpoint. Plan on walking three long blocks along Rossville Street (which becomes Lecky Road) to see them all. Locals are used to visitors and don't mind if you photograph the murals.

The best place to start is from William Street (opposite The People's Gallery), walking south along the right side of Rossville Street toward Free Derry Corner. The murals will all be on your right.

The first mural you'll walk past is the colorful ***Peace,*** showing the silhouette of a dove in flight (left side of mural) and an oak leaf (right side of mural), both created from a single ribbon. A peace campaign asked Derry city schoolchildren to write suggestions for positive peacetime images; their words inspired this artwork. The dove is a traditional symbol of peace, and the oak leaf is a traditional symbol of Derry—recognized by both communities. The dove flies from the sad blue of the past toward the warm yellow of the future.

Next, ***The Hunger Strikers*** features two long-haired figures wearing blankets. This mural represents the IRA prisoners who

refused to wear the uniforms of common criminal inmates in an attempt to force the British to treat them instead as legitimate political prisoners (who were allowed to wear their own clothes). The giant red letter *H* looms behind them, a symbol of the H-block layout of Maze Prison near Belfast.

Smaller and easy to miss (above a ramp with banisters) is ***John Hume.*** It's actually a collection of four faces (clockwise from upper left): Nationalist leader John Hume, Martin Luther King Jr., Nelson Mandela, and Mother Teresa. The Brooklyn Bridge in the middle symbolizes the long-term bridges of understanding that the work of these four Nobel Peace Prize-winning activists created. Born in the Bogside, Hume still maintains a home here.

Now look for ***The Saturday Matinee,*** which depicts an outgunned but undaunted local youth behind a screen shield. He holds a stone, ready to throw, while a British armored vehicle approaches (echoing the famous Tiananmen Square photo of the lone Chinese man facing the tank). Why *Saturday Matinee?* It's because the weekend was the best time for locals to "have a go at" the army; people were off work and kids were out of school.

Nearby is ***Civil Rights,*** showing a marching Derry crowd carrying an antisectarian banner. It dates from the days when Martin Luther King Jr.'s successful nonviolent marches were being seen worldwide on TV, creating a dramatic, global ripple effect. Civil rights marches, inspired by King and using the same methods to combat a similar set of grievances, gave this long-suffering community a powerful new voice.

DERRY

Political Murals

The dramatic and emotional murals you'll encounter in Northern Ireland will likely be one of the enduring travel memories that you'll take home with you. During the 19th century, Protestant neighborhoods hung flags and streamers each July to commemorate the victory of King William III at the Battle of the Boyne in 1690. Modern murals evolved from these colorful annual displays. With the advent of industrial paints, temporary seasonal displays became permanent territorial statements.

Unionist murals were created during the extended political debate that eventually led to the partitioning of the island in 1921, and the creation of Northern Ireland. Murals that expressed opposing views in Nationalist Catholic neighborhoods were outlawed. The ban remained until the eruption of the modern Troubles, when staunchly Nationalist Catholic communities isolated themselves behind barricades, eluding state control and gaining freedom to express their pent-up passions. In Derry, this form of symbolic, cultural, and ideological resistance first appeared in 1969 with the simple "You are now entering Free Derry" message that you'll still see painted on the surviving gable wall at Free Derry Corner.

Found mostly in working-class neighborhoods of Belfast and Derry, today's political murals have become a dynamic form of popular culture. They blur the line between art and propaganda, giving visitors a striking glimpse of each community's history, identity, and values.

In the building behind this mural, you'll find the small but passionate **Museum of Free Derry** (£3, Mon–Fri 9:30–16:30, plus April–Sept Sat 13:00–16:00 and July–Sept Sun 13:00–16:00, 55 Glenfada Park, tel. 028/7136-0880, www.museumoffreederry.org). Photos, shirts with bullet holes, and a 45-minute video documentary convey the painful experience of the people of the Bogside during the worst of the Troubles. Walking tours of the neighborhood depart from here daily at 10:00 and 14:00 (see "Tours in Derry").

Cross over to the other side of Rossville Street to see the **Bloody Sunday Monument.** This small, fenced-off stone obelisk lists the names of those who died that day, most within 50 yards of this spot. Take a look at the map pedestal by the monument, which shows how a rubble barricade was erected to block the street. A

10-story housing project called Rossville Flats stood here in those days. After peaceful protests failed (with Bloody Sunday being the watershed event), Nationalist youths became more aggressive. British troops were wary of being hit by Molotov cocktails thrown from the rooftop of the housing project.

Cross back again, this time over to the grassy median strip that runs down the middle of Rossville Street. At this end stands a granite letter *H* inscribed with the names of the 10 IRA hunger strikers who died in the H-block of Maze Prison in 1981. The prison was closed after the release of all prisoners (both Unionist and Nationalist) in 2000.

From here, as you look across at the corner of Fahan Street, you get a good view of two murals. In *The Runners* (right), three rioting youths flee tear gas from canisters used by the British Army to disperse hostile crowds. Over 1,000 canisters were used during the Battle of the Bogside; "nonlethal" rubber bullets killed 17 people over the course of the Troubles. Meanwhile, in *Operation Motorman* (left), a soldier wields a sledgehammer to break through a house door, depicting the massive push by the British Army to open up the Bogside's barricaded "no-go" areas that the IRA had controlled for three years (1969–1972).

Walk down to the other end of the median strip where the white wall of **Free Derry Corner** announces "You are now entering

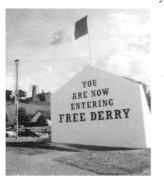

Free Derry" (imitating a similarly defiant slogan of the time in once-isolated West Berlin). This was once the gabled end of a string of houses that stood here almost 40 years ago. During the Troubles, it became a traditional meeting place for speakers to address crowds.

Cross back to the right side of the street (now Lecky Road) to see *Bloody Sunday,* in which a small group of men carry a body from that ill-fated march. It's based on a famous photo of Father Edward Daly that was taken that terrible day. Hunched over, he waves a white handkerchief to request safe passage in order to evacuate a mortally wounded protester. The blood-stained civil rights banner was inserted under the soldier's feet for extra emphasis. After Bloody Sunday, the previously marginal IRA suddenly found itself swamped with bitterly determined young recruits.

Near it is a mural called **Bernadette.** The woman with the megaphone is Bernadette Devlin McAliskey, an outspoken civil rights leader, who at age 21 became the youngest elected member of Parliament. Behind her kneels a female supporter, banging a trash-can lid against the street in a traditional expression of protest in Nationalist neighborhoods. Trash-can lids were also used to warn neighbors of the approach of British patrols.

Petrol Bomber, showing a teen wearing an army-surplus gas mask, captures the Battle of the Bogside, when locals barricaded their community, effectively shutting out British rule. Though the main figure's face is obscured by the mask, his body clearly communicates the resolve of an oppressed people. In the background, the long-gone Rossville Flats still looms, with an Irish tricolor flag flying from its top.

In **The Death of Innocence,** a young girl stands in front of bomb wreckage. She is Annette McGavigan, a 14-year-old who

was killed on this corner by crossfire in 1971. She was the 100th fatality of the Troubles, which eventually took more than 3,000 lives (and she's also a cousin of one of the artists). The broken gun beside her points to the ground, signifying that it's no longer being wielded. The large butterfly above her shoulder symbolizes the hope for peace. For years, the artists left the butterfly an empty silhouette until they felt confi-

dent that the peace process had succeeded. They finally filled in the butterfly with optimistic colors in the summer of 2006.

Finally, around the corner, you'll see a circle of male faces. This mural, painted in 1997 to observe the 25th anniversary of the tragedy, is called **Bloody Sunday Commemoration** and shows the 14 victims. They are surrounded by a ring of 14 oak leaves—the sym-

bol of Derry. When relatives of the dead learned that the three Bogside Artists were beginning to paint this mural, many came forward to loan the artists precious photos of their loved ones, so they could be more accurately depicted.

Take a few moments to walk into the **Bogside Inn** pub (facing this last mural across Westland Street). Order a drink and let your eyes adjust to the low light. This pub has been here through it all. Spend

a little time examining the black-and-white news photos of Bloody Sunday and bomb damage around the city, taken during the darkest days of Derry.

Sectarian violence eventually gave way to negotiations and a tenuous settlement. Nationalist leader John Hume (who shared the 1998 Nobel Peace Prize with Unionist leader David Trimble) once borrowed a quote from Gandhi to explain his nonviolent approach to the peace process: "An eye for an eye leaves everyone blind."

Sights in Derry

▲▲**Tower Museum Derry**—Housed in a modern reconstruction of a fortified medieval tower house that belonged to the local O'Doherty clan, this well-organized museum provides an excellent introduction to the city. Combining modern audiovisuals with historical artifacts, the displays tell the story of the city from a skillfully unbiased viewpoint, sorting out some of the tangled historical roots of Northern Ireland's Troubles. The museum is divided into two sections: The Story of Derry (on the ground floor) and the Spanish Armada (on the four floors of the tower).

Start with the Story of Derry, which explains the city's monastic origins 1,500 years ago. It moves through pivotal events, such as the 1688–1689 siege, as well as unexpected blips, like Amelia Earhart's emergency landing. Catch the thought-provoking 15-minute film in the small theater—it offers an evenhanded local perspective on the tragic events of the modern sectarian conflict, giving you a better handle on what makes this unique city tick. Scan the displays of paramilitary paraphernalia in the hallway lined with colored curbstones—red, white, and blue Union Jack colors for Unionists; and green, white, and orange Irish tricolor for Nationalists.

The tower section holds the Spanish Armada exhibits, filled with items taken from the wreck of *La Trinidad Valencera*. It sank in fierce storms nicknamed the "Protestant Winds" off the coast of Donegal in 1588 (£4 for all exhibits; July–Aug Mon–Sat 10:00–17:00, Sun 12:00–16:00; Sept–June Tue–Sat 10:00–17:00, closed Sun–Mon; Union Hall Place, tel. 028/7137-2411).

Guild Hall—This Neo-Gothic building, complete with clock tower, is the ceremonial seat of city government. It first opened in 1890 on reclaimed lands that were once the mudflats of the River Foyle. Destroyed by fire and rebuilt in 1913, it was massively damaged by IRA bombs in 1972. In an ironic twist, Gerry Doherty, one of those convicted of the bombings, was elected as a member of the Derry City Council a dozen years later. In November 1995, US President Bill Clinton spoke to thousands who packed into Guildhall Square. Inside the hall are the Council Chamber, party offices, and an assembly hall featuring stained-glass windows showing scenes from Derry history. Take an informational pamphlet from the front window and explore, if civic and cultural events are not taking place inside

(Mon–Fri 9:00–17:00, closed Sat–Sun, tel. 028/7137-7335).

Hands Across the Divide—Designed by local teacher Maurice Harron after the fall of the Iron Curtain, this powerful metal sculp-

ture of two figures extending their hands to each other was inspired by the growing hope for peace and reconciliation in Northern Ireland (located in a roundabout at the west end of Craigavon Bridge).

Until recently, the Tillie and Henderson's shirt factory (opened in 1857 and burned down in 2003) stood on the banks of the river beside the bridge, looming over the figures. In its heyday, Derry's

shirt industry employed more than 15,000 workers (90 percent of whom were women) in sweathouses typical of the human toll of the Industrial Revolution. Karl Marx mentioned this factory in *Das Kapital* as an example of women's transition from domestic to industrial work lives.

St. Columb's Cathedral—Marked by the tall spire inside the walls, this Anglican cathedral was built from 1628 to 1633 in a style called "Planter's Gothic." Its construction was financed by the same London companies that backed the Protestant plantation of Londonderry. It was the first Protestant cathedral built in Britain after the Reformation, and the cathedral played an important part in the defense of the city during the siege. During that time, cannons were mounted on its roof, and the original spire was scavenged for lead to melt into cannon shot. Before you enter, walk over to the "Heroes' Mound" at the end of the churchyard closest to the town wall. Underneath this grassy dome is a mass grave of some of those who died during the 1689 siege.

In the cathedral entryway, you'll find a hollow cannonball

that was lobbed into the city, containing the besiegers' surrender terms. Inside, along the nave, hangs a musty collection of battle flags and Union Jacks that once inspired troops during the siege, the Crimean War, and World War II. The American flag hangs among them, from the time when the first GIs to enter the European theater in World War II were based in Northern Ireland. Check out the small chapter-house museum in the back of the church to see the original locks of the gates of Derry and more relics of the siege (£2 donation, Mon–Sat 9:00–17:00, closed Sun, tel. 028/7126-7313, www.stcolumbscathedral.org).

Long Tower Church—Built below the walls on the hillside above the Bogside, this modest-looking church is worth a visit for its stunning high altar. The name comes from a stone monastic round tower that stood here for centuries but was dismantled and used for building materials in the 1600s. The oldest Catholic church in Derry, it was finished in 1786, during a time of enlightened relations between the city's two religious communities. Protestant Bishop Hervey gave a generous-for-the-time £200 donation, and had the four Corinthian columns shipped in from Naples to frame the Neo-Renaissance altar (free, usually open Mon–Sat 7:30–20:30, Sun 7:30–19:00—depending on available staff and church functions, tel. 028/7126-2301).

Hidden outside, behind the church and facing the Bogside, is a simple shrine beneath a hawthorn tree. It marks the spot where outlawed Masses were secretly held before this church was built, during the infamous Penal Law period of the early 1700s. Through the Penal Laws, the English attempted to weaken Catholicism's influence by banishing priests and forbidding Catholics from buying land, attending school, voting, and holding office.

Nightlife in Derry

The **Millennium Forum** is a modern venue that reflects the city's revived investment in local culture, concerts, and plays (box office open Mon–Sat 9:30–17:30, inside city walls on Newmarket Street near Ferryquay Gate, tel. 028/7126-4455, www.millenniumforum.co.uk, boxoffice@millenniumforum.co.uk).

The **Nerve Centre** shows a wide variety of art-house films and live concerts (inside city walls at 7–8 Magazine Street, near Butcher Gate, tel. 028/7126-0562, www.nerve-centre.org.uk).

Sleeping in Derry

$$$ Tower Hotel is the only hotel actually inside Derry's historic walls. It's a real splurge, with 93 modern and immaculate rooms, a classy bistro restaurant, and private basement parking (Sb-£57–99,

Sleep Code

(£1 = about $1.60, country code: 44, area code: 028)
S = Single, **D** = Double/Twin, **T** = Triple, **Q** = Quad, **b** = bathroom,
s = shower only. Breakfast is included and credit cards are
accepted unless otherwise noted.

    To help you easily sort through these listings, I've divided
the rooms into three categories, based on the price for a
standard double room with bath:

  $$$ **Higher Priced**—Most rooms £80 or more.
   $$ **Moderately Priced**—Most rooms between £40–80.
    $ **Lower Priced**—Most rooms £40 or less.

Db-£64–110, online deals, Butcher Street, tel. 028/7137-1000, fax 028/7137-1234, www.towerhotelderry.com, reservations@thd.ie).

$$ Travelodge has 44 comfortable rooms, a great location, and a handy adjacent parking garage (Db-£50 Sun–Thu, Db-£60–85 Fri–Sat, significant online discounts if you book ahead, continental breakfast-£6, 22–24 Strand Road, tel. 028/7127-1271, fax 028/7127-1277, www.travelodge.ie).

$$ Merchant's House, on a quiet street a 10-minute stroll from Waterloo Place, is a fine Georgian townhouse with a grand, colorful drawing room and eight rooms sporting marble fireplaces and ornate plasterwork (Sb-£40–45, Db-£60–65, closed Jan–Feb, Wi-Fi, 16 Queen Street, tel. 028/7126-9691, fax 028/7126-6913, www.thesaddlershouse.com, saddlershouse@btinternet.com, Joan and Peter Pyne also run the Saddler's House, below).

$$ Saddler's House, run by the owners of Merchant's House, is a charming Victorian townhouse with seven rooms located a couple of blocks closer to the old town walls (Sb-£40-45, Db-£60-65, closed Jan–Feb, Wi-Fi, 36 Great James Street, tel. 028/7126-9691, fax 028/7126-6913, www.thesaddlershouse.com, saddlershouse @btinternet.com).

$ Paddy's Palace Hostel, located in the city center, rents 40 decent beds for £12–13 a night with breakfast. Look for the green-and-yellow building, and pause to read the great Mark Twain quote above the front door (4 to 6 beds per room, family rooms with private bathroom for up to four-£50, Internet access, laundry facilities, kitchen, 1 Woodleigh Terrace, Asylum Road, tel. 028/7130-9051, www.paddyspalace.com, steve@irishexperience .ie, Stephen McPhilemy). Ask about their adjacent self-catering apartments. Stephen also offers walking tours (see "Tours in Derry").

Eating in Derry

The **Mandarin Palace** dishes up good £10–13 Chinese dinners in a crisp dining room facing the river (daily 16:30–23:00, buffet lunch Mon–Fri 12:00–14:00, £10 early-bird two-course deals 16:30–19:00, Queens Quay at Lower Clarendon Street, tel. 028/7137-3656).

The hip, trendy **Exchange Restaurant and Wine Bar** offers £7–9 lunches and quality £12–16 dinners with flair, in a central location near the river behind Waterloo Place (Mon–Sat 12:00–14:30 & 17:30–22:00, Sun 16:00–21:00, Queen's Quay, tel. 028/7127-3990).

Easygoing **Fitzroy's,** tucked below Ferryquay Gate, serves good £7–10 lunches and £9–15 dinners (Mon–Sat 12:00–22:00, Sun 13:00–20:00, 2–4 Bridge Street, tel. 028/7126-6211).

The **Bay Leaf,** a local hangout close to my recommended hotels, has basic but hearty lunch and dinner options (Tue–Fri 12:00–14:30 & 17:30–21:45, Sat 17:30–21:45, Sun 16:00–21:00, closed Mon, 2 Clarendon Street, tel. 028/7126-0987).

Austins Department Store, right on the Diamond in the center of the old city, is Ireland's oldest department store (1830) and has a top-floor café with some lofty views and £5 lunch specials (Mon–Sat 9:30–17:30, Sun 13:00–17:00, 2–6 The Diamond, tel. 028/7126-1817).

Chat with locals in pubs that rarely see a tourist. Try **Peadar O'Donnell's** pub on Waterloo Street for Derry's best nightly traditional-music sessions (53 Waterloo Street, tel. 028/7137-2318).

Supermarkets: **Tesco** has everything for picnics and road munchies (Mon–Thu 9:00–21:00, Fri 8:30–21:00, Sat 8:30–20:00, Sun 13:00–18:00, corner of Strand Road and Clarendon Street). **SuperValu** meets the same needs (Mon–Wed 8:30–18:30, Thu–Fri until 20:00, Sat 8:30–18:00, closed Sun, Waterloo Place).

Derry Connections

From Derry, it's less than an hour's drive to Portrush. If you're using public transportation, consider getting a £15 "Day Tracker" ticket, good for all-day train and bus use in Northern Ireland. Useful updated schedules and prices for both trains and buses in Northern Ireland can be obtained from Translink (tel. 028/9066-6630, www.translink.co.uk). Keep in mind that some bus and train schedules, road signs, and maps may say "Londonderry" or "L'Derry" instead of "Derry."

From Derry by Train to: Portrush (9/day, 1.5 hrs, change in Coleraine), **Belfast** (9/day, 2.5 hrs), **Dublin** (7/day, 5 hrs).

By Bus to: Galway (4/day, 6 hrs), **Portrush** (5/day, 1.25 hrs), **Belfast** (20/day, 1.75 hrs), **Dublin** (5/day, 4.5 hrs).

For Drivers: Northern Ireland Sights Between Derry and Galway

If you're driving into Northern Ireland from Galway, Westport, or Strokestown and don't have time to explore Donegal, consider these two interesting stops in the interior.

Belleek Pottery Visitors Centre—Just over the Northern Ireland border (30 miles northeast of Sligo) is the cute town of Belleek, famous for its pottery. The Belleek Parian China factory welcomes visitors with a small gallery and museum (Mon–Fri 9:00–17:30, Sat 10:00–17:30, Sun 12:00–17:30, less off-season), a 20-minute video, a cheery cafeteria, and fascinating 30-minute tours of its working factory (£4, open April–June and Sept Mon–Fri 9:00–17:30, Sat 10:00–17:30, Sun 14:00–18:00; longer hours July–Aug, shorter hours Oct–March, closed Sun Nov–March; no tours Sat–Sun; call to confirm schedule and reserve a spot, tel. 028/6865-8501, www.belleek.ie). Crazed shoppers who forget to fill out a VAT tax

refund form will find their financial situation looking Belleek.

▲Ulster American Folk Park—North of Omagh (five miles on A-5), this combination museum and folk park commemorates the many Irish who left their homeland during the hard times of the 19th century. Exhibits show life before emigration, on the boat, and in America. You'll gain insight into the origins of the tough Scotch-Irish stock—think Davy Crockett (his folk were from Derry) and Andrew Jackson (Carrickfergus roots)—who later shaped America's westward migration (£5.50; April–Sept Mon–Sat 10:30–16:30, Sun 11:00–17:00; Oct–March Mon–Fri 10:30–15:30, closed Sat–Sun; cafeteria, tel. 028/8224-3292, www.folkpark.com).

The adjacent **Centre for Migration Studies** is handy for genealogy searches (Mon–Fri 10:30–17:00, closed Sat–Sun, tel. 028/8225-6315, www.qub.ac.uk/cms).

County Donegal

Donegal is the most remote (and perhaps the most ruggedly beautiful) county in Ireland. It's not on the way to anywhere, and it wears this isolation well. With more native Irish speakers than in any other county, the old ways are better preserved here. The northernmost part of Ireland, Donegal remains connected to the Republic by a slim, five-mile-wide umbilical cord of land on its southern coast. It's also Ireland's second-biggest county, with a wide-open "big sky" interior and a shattered-glass, 200-mile, jagged coastline of islands and inlets.

This is the home turf of St. Colmcille (St. Columba in English; means "dove of the church" in Irish), who was born here in 521. In the hierarchy of revered Irish saints, he's second only to St. Patrick. A proud Gaelic culture held out in Donegal to the bitter end, when its two famous clans (the O'Donnells and the O'Dohertys) were finally defeated by the English in the early 1600s. After their defeat, the region became known as Dun na nGall ("the fort of the foreigner"), which was eventually anglicized to Donegal.

As the English moved in, four friars (certain that Gaelic ways would be lost forever) painstakingly wrote down Irish history from Noah's Ark to their present. This labor of love became known as the Annals of the Four Masters, and without it, much of our knowledge of early Irish history and myth would have been lost. An obelisk stands in their honor in the main square of Donegal town.

The hardy people of County Donegal were famous for their quality tweed weaving, a cottage industry that has given way to modern industrial production in far-off cities. An energetic fishing fleet still churns offshore. The traditional Irish musicians of Donegal play a driving style of music with a distinctively fast and choppy rhythm. Meanwhile, Enya (local Gweedore gal made good) has crafted languid, ethereal tunes that glide from mood to mood. Both *Dancing at Lughnasa* and *The Secret of Roan Inish* were filmed in County Donegal. Today, emigration has taken its toll, and the region relies on a trickle of tourism spilling over from Northern Ireland.

Sights in Donegal

Donegal Loop Trip

Here's my choice for a scenic mix of Donegal highlands and coastal views, organized as a daylong circuit (150 miles) for drivers based across the border in Derry. If you're coming north from Galway or Westport, you could incorporate parts of this drive into your itinerary.

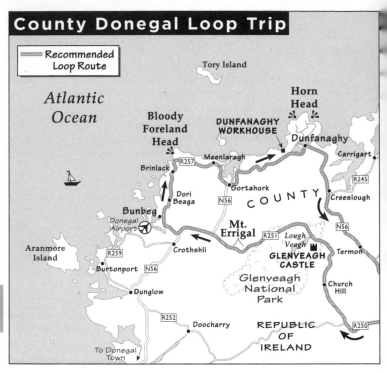

Route Summary: Drive west out of Derry (direction: Letterkenny) on Buncrana Road, which becomes A-2 (and then N-13 across the border in the Republic). Follow the signs into Letterkenny, and take R-250 out the other (west) end of town. Veer right (north) onto R-251, and stay on it through Church Hill, all the way across the highlands, until you link up with N-56 approaching Bunbeg. After a couple of miles on N-56, take R-258 another four miles into Bunbeg. Depart Bunbeg going north on R-257, around Bloody Foreland, and rejoin N-56 near Gortahork. Take N-56 through Dunfanaghy (possible Horn Head mini-loop option here), and then south, back into Letterkenny. Retrace your route from Letterkenny via N-13 and A-2 back into Derry.

Helpful Hints: An early start and an Ordnance Survey map are essential. It's cheapest to top off your gas tank in Letterkenny. Consider bringing along a picnic lunch to enjoy from a scenic roadside pullout along the Bloody Foreland R-257 road, or out on the Horn Head loop. Bring your camera and remember—not all who wander are lost.

Once you cross into the Republic of Ireland, all currency is in euros, not pounds. For B&B rates, entry fees, and all other costs in Donegal, keep this exchange rate in mind: €1 = about $1.40.

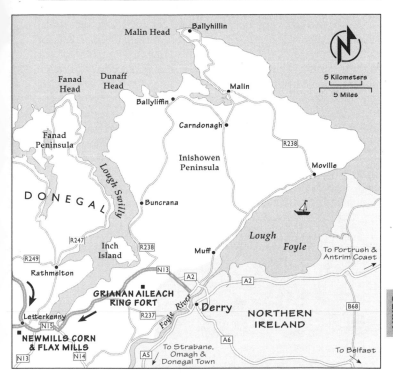

The sights (listed next) along this route are well-marked. Don't underestimate the time it takes to get around here, as the narrow roads are full of curves and bumps. Dogs, bred to herd sheep, dart from side lanes to practice their bluffing techniques on the reflection in your hubcaps. If you average 30 miles per hour over the course of the day, you've got a very good suspension system. Folks wanting to linger at more than a couple of sights will need to slow down and consider an overnight stop in Bunbeg or Dunfanaghy.

Grianan Aileach Ring Fort

This dramatic, ancient ring fort perches on an 800-foot hill just inside the Republic, a stone's throw from Derry. It's an Iron Age

fortification, built about the time of Christ, and was once the royal stronghold of the O'Neill clan, which dominated Ulster for centuries. Its stout, drystone walls (no mortar) are 12 feet thick and 18 feet high, creating an interior sanctuary 80 feet in diameter (entry is free and unattended).

Once inside, you can scramble up the stairs, built into the walls, to enjoy panoramic views in all directions. Murtagh O'Brien, King of Desmond, destroyed the fort in 1101 (the same year he gave the Rock of Cashel to the Church). He had each of his soldiers carry away one stone to make it tougher for the O'Neill clan to find the raw materials to rebuild. What you see today is mostly a reconstruction from the 1870s. You'll see a sign for the fort posted on N-13, not far from the junction of R-239. Turn up the steep hill at the modern church with the round roof, and follow signs two miles (3 km) to the fort.

Newmills Corn and Flax Mills

Come here for a glimpse of the 150-year-old Industrial Revolution, shown high-tech Ulster style. Linen, which comes from flax, was

king in this region. The 15-minute film does a nifty job of explaining the process, showing how the common flax plant ends up as cloth. Working conditions in a mill were noisy, unhealthy, and exhausting. Veteran mill workers often braved respiratory disease, deafness, lost fingers, and extreme fire danger. For their trouble, they usually got to keep about 10 percent of what they milled.

The corn mill is still in working condition, but requires a skilled miller to operate it. This mill ground oats—"corn" means oats in Ireland. (What we call corn, they call maize.) The huge waterwheel, powered by the River Swilly, made five revolutions per minute and generated eight horsepower.

The entire operation could be handled by one miller, who knew every cog, lever, and flume in the joint. Call ahead to see when working mill demonstrations are scheduled; otherwise, tours last 20 minutes and are available on request (free, June–Sept daily 10:00–18:00, last entry 15 min before closing, closed off-season, 5 miles west of Letterkenny on R-250, Churchill Road, tel. 074/912-5115).

Glenveagh Castle and National Park

One of Ireland's six national parks, Glenveagh's jewel is pristine Lough Veagh (Loch Ghleann Bheatha in Gaelic). The lake is three miles long, occupying a U-shaped valley scoured out of the Derryveagh mountains by powerful glaciers during the last ice age.

Donegal or Bust

Part of western County Donegal is in the Gaeltacht, where locals speak the Irish (Gaelic) language. In the spring of 2005, a controversial law was passed that erased all English place names from local road signs in Gaeltacht areas. Signs now only have the Irish-language equivalent, an attempt to protect the region from the further (and inevitable) encroachment by the English language.

Here's a cheat sheet to help you decipher the signs as you drive the Donegal loop (parts of which are in the Gaeltacht). There's also a complete translation of all Irish place names in the recommended *Complete Road Atlas of Ireland* by Ordnance Survey (€13), in the Gazetteer section in the back.

Gaelic Name	Pronounced	English Name
Leitir Ceanainn	*LET-ir CAN-ning*	Letterkenny
Min an Labain	*MEEN on law-BAWN*	Churchill
Loch Ghleann Bheatha	*LOCKH thown eh-VEH-heh*	Lough (Lake) Veagh
An Earagail	*on AIR-i-gul*	Mt. Errigal
Gaoth Dobhair	*GWEE door*	Gweedore
Crothshli	*CROTH-lee*	Crolly
Bun Beag	*bun bee-OWG*	Bunbeg
Dori Beaga	*DOR-uh bee-OWG-uh*	Derrybeg
Cnoc Fola	*NOK FAW-luh*	Bloody Foreland
Gort an Choirce	*gurt on HER-kuh*	Gortahork
Dun Fionnachaidh	*doon on-AH-keh*	Dunfanaghy
Corran Binne	*COR-on BIN-eh*	Horn Head

In the 1850s, this scenic area attracted the wealthy land speculator John George Adair, who bought the valley in 1857. Right away, Adair clashed with local tenants, whom he accused of stealing his sheep. After his managing agent was found murdered, he evicted all 244 of his bitter tenants to great controversy, and set about to create a hunting estate in grand Victorian style.

His pride and joy was his country mansion, Glenveagh Castle, finished in 1873 on the shore of Lough Veagh. After his death, his widow added to the castle and introduced rhododendrons and rare red deer to the estate. After her death, Harvard art professor Kingsley Porter bought the estate, and promptly disappeared on the Donegal coast. (He's thought to have drowned.) The last owner was Philadelphia millionaire Henry McIlhenny, who filled the mansion with fine art and furniture while perfecting the lush surrounding gardens. He donated the castle to the Irish nation in 1981.

Take the 45-minute castle tour, letting your Jane Austen and Agatha Christie fantasies go wild. Antlers abound on walls, in chandeliers, and in paintings by Victorian hunting artists. A table crafted from rare bog oak (from ancient trees hundreds of years old, found buried in the muck) stands at attention in one room, while Venetian glass chandeliers illuminate a bathroom. A round pink bedroom at the top of a tower is decorated in Oriental style, with inlaid mother-of-pearl furnishings. The library, which displays paintings by George Russell, has the castle's best lake views.

Afterward, stroll through the gardens and enjoy the lovely setting. A lakeside swimming pool had boilers underneath it to keep it heated. It's no wonder that Greta Garbo was an occasional guest, coming to visit whenever she "vanted" to be alone.

The castle is only accessible by 10-minute shuttle-bus rides (€2, 4/hr, depart from the park visitors center, last shuttle at 17:00). The visitors center, located beside the parking lot and tearoom, explains the region's natural history. Hiking trails in the park are tempting, but beware of tiny midges that seem to want to nest in your nostrils (€3, covered by Heritage Card, mid-March–early Nov daily 10:00–18:00, last admission 17:00, early Nov–mid-March Sat–Sun only, tel. 074/913-7090).

Without a car, you can reach Glenveagh Castle and National Park by bus tour from Derry (see "Tours in Derry").

Mount Errigal (An Earagail)

The mountain (2,400 feet) dominates the horizon for miles around. Rising from the relatively flat interior bog land, it looks taller from a distance than it is. Beautifully cone-shaped (but not a volcano), it offers a hearty nontechnical climb with panoramic views (4 hours round-trip, covering 5 miles). Hikers should ask for a weather report (frequent mists squat on the summit). The trailhead is southeast of the moun-

tain, starting at the small parking lot right beside R-251 on the lower slope of the mountain (easy to spot, with a low surrounding stone wall in middle of open bog land).

Bunbeg (Bun Beag)

This modest town lies along R-257 and offers a fine sandy beach. But take the trouble to seek out the quaint, hidden fishing harbor at the rocky south end of town. The harbor-access road is directly in front of you as you approach the town from the east on R-258 and pull up to the stop sign where R-258 meets R-257. At the dead end of the half-mile access road is a cute, watercolor-worthy harbor, with an old stone warehouse and a great guesthouse (described below).

There's an ATM at the AIB bank (on the left, going north on R-257, 100 yards past Seaview Hotel). The post office is in the back of the tiny Macaire Clocair market (Mon–Sat 9:00–17:30, Sat 9:00–13:00, closed Sun).

Turasmara operates a limited ferry service from Bunbeg harbor. It's a 90-minute voyage to the ultra-remote and rugged Tory Island (€25–round-trip, runs daily June–Sept—weather permitting, departs at 9:00 and returns at 18:00, call to confirm schedule, tel. 074/953-1340). Active travelers will enjoy the invigorating and scenic Rib Boat Excursions, which depart from Bunbeg House on the shore of cozy Bunbeg harbor and weave among the nearby islands (€20, 45 min, daily mid-June–Aug, 10 people per boat, call for schedule, tel. 074/953-1305, www.bunbeghouse.com).

Sleeping in Bunbeg: **$$ Bunbeg House,** overlooking the snug and charming Bunbeg fishing harbor, has 12 simple, spacious rooms and a tiny, inviting pub downstairs. Andy and Jean Carr know about fun rib-boat sightseeing excursions, too (Sb-€45–50, Db-€75–85, Tb-€95–110, Qb-€120, parking, tel. 074/953-1305, fax 074/953-1420, www.bunbeghouse.com, bunbeghouse@eircom.net).

$$ Teach Anraoi B&B is a comfortable home with five clean, economical, unpretentious rooms (Sb-€30, Db-€55, cash only, non-smoking; on R-257 in the middle of Bunbeg, 100 yards past the bank, down a steep driveway; tel. 074/953-1092, Roisin Gallagher).

Eating in Bunbeg: Try the **Seaview Hotel Bistro,** which specializes in fish dishes (€24–28 meals, June–Sept daily 18:30–21:00, Oct–May Fri–Sat only 18:30–21:00, on R-257, tel. 074/953-1159). You'll find a fine pub dinner, plus late-evening traditional-music sessions nightly, at **Leo's Tavern,** run by Enya's dad. To get there from Bunbeg, hop on N-56 going south through the nearby hamlet of Crolly. Take a right onto R-259 (sign says *Aerphort*), and go a half-mile, following signs to Leo's, which will bring you to a jackknife—turn right and the pub is 100 yards up on the left (Mon–Sat 13:00–20:30, Sun 13:00–15:30, tel. 074/954-8143). Groceries are sold at the **Spar Market** in nearby Derrybeg (Mon–Sat 9:00–19:30, Sun 9:00–13:30).

From Bunbeg to Derrybeg (Dori Beaga): The five miles of road heading north—as Bunbeg blends into Derrybeg (and a bit beyond)—are some of the most densely populated sections of this loop tour. Modern holiday cottages pepper the landscape in what the Irish have come to call "Bungalow Bliss" (or "Bungalow Blight" to nature-lovers).

Bloody Foreland (Cnoc Fola)

Named for the shade of red that backlit heather turns at sunset, this scenic headland is laced with rock walls and forgotten cottage ruins. Pull off at one of the lofty roadside viewpoints and savor a picnic lunch and rugged coastal views.

Dunfanaghy Workhouse

Opened in 1845, this structure was part of an extensive workhouse compound (separating families by gender and age)—a dreaded last resort for the utterly destitute of coastal Donegal. There were once many identical compounds built across Ireland, a rigid Victorian solution to the spiraling riddle of Ireland's rapidly multiplying poor. But the system was unable to cope with the starving, homeless multitudes who were victims of the famine.

The harsh workhouse experience is told through the true-life narrative of Wee Hannah Herrity, a wandering orphan and former resident of this workhouse. She survived the famine by taking refuge here, and died at age 90 in 1926. You'll visit three upstairs rooms where hokey papier-mâché figures relate the powerful episodes in her life (€4.50, April–Sept Mon–Sat 10:00–16:00, closed Sun; Oct–March Sat–Sun only; call to confirm winter hours, good bookstore and coffee shop, on N-56 a half-mile south of Dunfanaghy town, tel. 074/913-6540, www.dunfanaghywork house.ie).

Dunfanaghy (Dun Fionnachaidh)

This planned town, founded by the English in the early 1600s for local markets and fairs, has a prim and proper appearance. In Dunfanaghy (dun-FAN-ah-hee), you can grab a pub lunch or some picnic fixings from the town market. Enjoy them from a scenic viewpoint on the nearby Horn Head loop drive (described later).

The post office is at the southern end of town (Mon–Fri 9:00–17:30, Sat 9:00–13:00, closed Sun). Basic groceries are sold in **Ramsay's Store** (daily 7:30–21:30) on the pier opposite the Muck & Muffin.

Sleeping in Dunfanaghy: **$$$ The Mill Restaurant and Accommodation** is a diamond in the Donegal rough. Susan Alcorn nurtures six wonderful rooms with classy decor, while her husband Derek is the chef in their fine restaurant downstairs (Sb-€75, Db-€100–105, Tb-€135, non-smoking, parking, tel. & fax 074/913-6985, www.themillrestaurant.com, info@themill restaurant.com).

\$\$ The Whins B&B has tastefully exotic furnishings in its four prim rooms (Sb-€40–50, Db-€70–75, Tb-€90–105, non-smoking, parking, 10-min walk north of town, tel. 074/913-6481, www.thewhins.com, annemarie@thewhins.com, Anne-Marie Moore).

Eating in Dunfanaghy: **The Mill Restaurant and Accommodation** is gourmet all the way, specializing in memorable lamb or lobster dinners worth booking days ahead of time (€45, Tue–Sun 19:00–21:00, closed Mon, tel. 074/913-6985). **Muck & Muffin** is a simple sandwich café, great for quick, cheap lunches. It's above the pottery shop in the stone warehouse on the town square (Mon–Sat 9:30–17:00, mid-June–mid-Sept until 21:00; Sun 11:00–17:00; tel. 074/913-6780).

Horn Head Loop (Corran Binne)

If you have extra time, take an hour as you approach Dunfanaghy to embark on a lost-world plateau drive. This heaving headland

with few trees has gripping coastal views. Consult your map and get off N-56, following the Horn Head signs all the way around the eastern lobe of the peninsula. There's less than eight miles of narrow, single-lane road out here, with very little traffic. But be alert and willing to pull over at wide spots to cooperate with other cars.

This stone-studded peninsula was once an island. Then, shortly after the last ice age ended, ocean currents deposited a sandy spit in the calm water behind the island. A hundred years ago, locals harvested its stabilizing dune grass, using it for roof thatching, and sending it abroad to Flanders for soldiers to create beds for horses during World War I. However, with the grass gone, the sandy spit was free to migrate again. It promptly silted up the harbor, created a true peninsula, and ruined Dunfanaghy as a port town.

A short spur road leads to the summit of the headland, where you can park your car and walk another 50 yards up to the abandoned lookout shelter. The views from here are dramatic, looking west toward Tory Island and south to Mount Errigal. Some may choose to hike an additional 30 minutes across the heather, to the ruins of the distant signal tower (not a castle), clearly visible near the cliffs. The trails are not maintained, but it's easy bushwhacking, offering rewarding cliff views. Navigate back to your car, using the lookout shelter on the summit as a landmark.

DERRY

PRACTICALITIES

This section covers just the basics on traveling in Northern Ireland (for much more information, see *Rick Steves' Ireland 2010*). You can find free advice on specific topics at www.ricksteves.com/tips.

While it shares an island with the Republic of Ireland, Northern Ireland is part of the United Kingdom—which makes its currency, phone codes, and other practicalities different from the Republic. Keep in mind that County Donegal, described in this book as a handy side-trip from Derry, is actually in the Republic of Ireland.

Money

For currency, Northern Ireland uses the pound (£): 1 pound (£1) = about $1.60. One pound is broken into 100 pence (p). To convert prices in pounds to dollars, add about 60 percent: £20 = about $32, £50 = about $80. (Check www.oanda.com for the latest exchange rates.) While the pound used here is called the "Ulster Pound," it's interchangeable with the British pound. Note that County Donegal, in the Republic of Ireland, uses euros (€1 = about $1.40).

The standard way for travelers to get local currency is to withdraw money from a cash machine using a debit or credit card, ideally with a Visa or MasterCard logo. Before departing, call your bank or credit-card company: Confirm that your card will work overseas, ask about international transaction fees, and alert them that you'll be making withdrawals in Europe.

To keep your valuables safe, wear a money belt. But if you do lose your credit or debit card, report the loss immediately to the respective global customer-assistance centers. Call these 24-hour US numbers collect: Visa (410/581-9994), MasterCard (636/722-7111), and American Express (623/492-8427).

Phoning

Smart travelers use the telephone to reserve or reconfirm rooms, reserve restaurants, get directions, research transportation connections, confirm tour times, phone home, and lots more.

To call Northern Ireland from the US or Canada: Dial 011-44 and then 28 (Northern Ireland's area code, minus its initial zero), followed by the local number. (The 011 is our international access code, and 44 is the UK's country code.)

To call Northern Ireland from a European country: Dial 00-44 followed by 28 and the local number. (The 00 is Europe's international access code.)

To call within Northern Ireland and the UK: Since all of Northern Ireland shares one area code (028), all calls within the country are local—so you can leave off the area code and simply dial the local number. If you're calling to or from elsewhere in the UK, you need to include the area code.

Calling between Northern Ireland and the Republic of Ireland: To make calls from Northern Ireland to the Republic, dial 00-353, then the area code without its initial 0, then the local number. To call from the Republic to Northern Ireland, dial 048, then the local number (without the 028 area code).

To call from Northern Ireland to another country: Dial 00 followed by the country code (for example, 1 for the US or Canada), then the area code and number. If you're calling European countries whose phone numbers begin with 0, you'll usually have to omit that 0 when you dial.

Tips on Phoning: To make calls in Northern Ireland, you can buy two different types of phone cards—international or insertable—sold locally at newsstands. Cheap international phone cards, which work with a scratch-to-reveal PIN code at any phone, allow you to call home to the US for pennies a minute, and also work for domestic calls within Northern Ireland. Insertable phone cards, which must be inserted into public pay phones, are reasonable for calls within Northern Ireland (and work for international calls as well, but not as cheaply as the international phone cards). Calling from your hotel-room phone is usually expensive, unless you use an international phone card. A mobile phone—whether an American one that works in Northern Ireland, or a European one you buy when you arrive—is handy, but can be pricey. For more on phoning, see www.ricksteves.com/phoning.

Emergency Telephone Numbers in Northern Ireland: To summon the **police** or an **ambulance,** dial 999. For passport problems, call the **US Embassy** (in Belfast, tel. 028/9038-6100) or the **Canadian Embassy** (in Belfast, tel. 028/9127-2060). For other concerns, get advice from your hotel.

Making Hotel and B&B Reservations

To ensure the best value, I recommend reserving rooms in advance, particularly during peak season. Email the hotelier or B&B host with the following key pieces of information: number and type of rooms; number of nights; date of arrival; date of departure; and any special requests. (For a sample form, see www.ricksteves.com/reservation.) Use the European style for writing dates: day/month/year. For example, for a two-night stay in July, you could request: "1 double room for 2 nights, arrive 16/07/10, depart 18/07/10." Hoteliers typically ask for your credit-card number as a deposit.

Know the terminology: An "en suite" room has a bathroom (toilet and shower/tub) actually inside the room; a room with a "private bathroom" can mean that the bathroom is all yours, but it's across the hall; and a "standard" room has access to a bathroom that's shared with other rooms and down the hall.

In these times of economic uncertainty, some hotels are willing to deal to attract guests—try emailing several to ask their best rate. In general, hotel prices can soften if you do any of the following: stay in a "standard" room, offer to pay cash, stay at least three nights, or travel off-season.

Eating

The traditional "Ulster Fry" breakfast, which is usually included at your B&B or hotel, consists of juice, tea or coffee, cereal, eggs, bacon, sausage, toast, a grilled tomato, sautéed mushrooms, and black pudding. If it's too much for you, order only the items you want.

To dine affordably at classier restaurants, look for "early-bird specials" (offered about 17:30–19:00, last order by 19:00). At a sit-down place with table service, tip about 10 percent—unless the service charge is already listed on the bill.

Smart travelers use pubs (short for "public houses") to eat, drink, and make new friends. Pub grub is Northern Ireland's best eating value. For about $15–20, you'll get a basic hot lunch or dinner. The menu is hearty and traditional: stews, soups, fish-and-chips, meat, cabbage, potatoes, and—in coastal areas—fresh seafood. Order drinks and meals at the bar. Pay as you order, and don't tip.

Most pubs have lagers (cold, refreshing, American-style beer), ales (amber-colored, cellar-temperature beer), bitters (hop-flavored ale, perhaps the most typical British beer), and stouts (dark and somewhat bitter—the most famous is Guinness, of course).

Transportation

By Car: A car is a worthless headache in Belfast. But if venturing into the countryside, I enjoy the freedom of a rental car for reaching far-flung rural sights. It's cheaper to arrange most car rentals from the US. For tips on your insurance options, see www.ricksteves.com/cdw. (If you're also going to the Republic of Ireland, note that many credit-card companies do not offer collision coverage for rentals in the Republic.) Bring your driver's license. For route planning, try www.viamichelin.com.

Remember that people throughout Ireland drive on the left side of the road (and the driver sits on the right side of the car). You'll quickly master the many roundabouts: Traffic moves clockwise, cars inside the roundabout have the right-of-way, and entering traffic yields (look to your right as you merge). Note that "camera cops" strictly enforce speed limits by automatically snapping photos of speeders' license plates, then mailing them a bill.

By Train and Bus: The best overall source for public transportation schedules is the Tourism Ireland website: www.discover ireland.com (select "Plan Your Visit," then "Getting Around"). You can also check train and bus schedules at www.translink. co.uk, or call 028/9066-6630. To see if a railpass could save you money, check www.ricksteves.com/rail.

Long-distance buses (called "coaches") are about a third slower than trains, but they're also much cheaper. Bus stations are normally at or near train stations.

Helpful Hints

Time: Northern Ireland uses the 24-hour clock. It's the same through 12:00 noon, then keep going: 13:00, 14:00, and so on. Ireland, like Great Britain, is five/eight hours ahead of the East/West Coasts of the US (and one hour earlier than most of continental Europe).

Holidays and Festivals: Northern Ireland celebrates many holidays, which can close sights and attract crowds (book hotel rooms ahead). For information on holidays and festivals, check Ireland's website: www.discoverireland.com. For a simple list showing major—though not all—events, see www.ricksteves.com/festivals.

Numbers and Stumblers: What Americans call the second floor of a building is the first floor in Northern Ireland. Local people write dates as day/month/year, so Christmas is 25/12/10. For most measurements, Northern Ireland uses the metric system: A kilogram is 2.2 pounds, and a liter is about a quart. For driving distances, they use miles (though the Republic is transitioning to kilometers).

Resources from Rick Steves

This Snapshot guide is excerpted from *Rick Steves' Ireland 2010*, which is one of more than 30 titles in my series of guidebooks on European travel. I also produce a public television series, *Rick Steves' Europe,* and a public radio show, *Travel with Rick Steves.* My website, www.ricksteves.com, offers free travel information, free vodcasts and podcasts of my shows, free audio tours of major sights in Europe (for you to download onto an iPod or other MP3 player), a Graffiti Wall for travelers' comments, guidebook updates, my travel blog, an online travel store, and information on European railpasses and our tours of Europe.

Additional Resources
Tourist Information: www.discoverireland.com
Passports and Red Tape: www.travel.state.gov
Packing List: www.ricksteves.com/packlist
Cheap Flights: www.skyscanner.net
Airplane Carry-on Restrictions: www.tsa.gov/travelers
Updates for This Book: www.ricksteves.com/update

How Was Your Trip?
If you'd like to share your tips, concerns, and discoveries after using this book, please fill out the survey at www.ricksteves.com/feedback. Thanks in advance—it helps a lot.

PRACTICALITIES

Rick Steves ®
EUROPEAN TOURS

ADRIATIC • ATHENS & THE HEART OF GREECE • BARCELONA & MADRID • BELGIUM & HOLLAND • BERLIN, VIENNA & PRAGUE BEST OF EUROPE • BEST OF ITALY BEST OF TURKEY • BULGARIA • EASTERN EUROPE • ENGLAND • FAMILY EUROPE GERMANY, AUSTRIA & SWITZERLAND HEART OF ITALY • IRELAND • ISTANBUL LONDON • PARIS • PARIS & HEART OF FRANCE • PARIS & SOUTH OF FRANCE PORTUGAL • PRAGUE & BUDAPEST • ROME SAN SEBASTIAN & BASQUE COUNTRY SCANDINAVIA • SCOTLAND • SICILY SOUTH ITALY • SPAIN & MOROCCO ST. PETERSBURG, TALLINN & HELSINKI VENICE, FLORENCE & ROME • VILLAGE FRANCE • VILLAGE ITALY • VILLAGE TURKEY

VISIT **TOURS.RICKSTEVES.COM**

Great guides, small groups, no grumps

▶ Plan Your Trip

Browse thousands of articles and a wealth of money-saving tips for planning your dream trip. You'll find up-to-date information on Europe's best destinations, packing smart, getting around, finding rooms, staying healthy, avoiding scams and more.

▶ Eurail Passes

Find out, step-by-step, if a rail pass makes sense for your trip—and how to avoid buying more than you need. Get a bunch of free extras!

▶ Graffiti Wall & Travelers' Helpline

Learn, ask, share—our online community of savvy travelers is a great resource for first-time travelers to Europe, as well as seasoned pros.

Rick Steves' Europe Through the Back Door, Inc.

NOW AVAILABLE

RICK STEVES APPS FOR THE iPHONE OR iPOD TOUCH

With these apps you can:

► Spin the compass icon to switch views between sights, hotels, and restaurant selections—and get details on cost, hours, address, and phone number.

► Tap any point on the screen to read Rick's detailed information, including history and suggested viewpoints.

► Get a deeper view into Rick's tours with audio and video segments.

Go to iTunes to download the following apps:

Rick Steves' Louvre Tour

Rick Steves' Historic Paris Walk

Rick Steves' Orsay Museum Tour

Rick Steves' Versailles

Rick Steves' Ancient Rome Tour

Rick Steves' St. Peter's Basilica Tour

Once downloaded, these apps are completely self-contained on your iPhone or iPod Touch, so you will not incur pricey roaming charges during use overseas.

Rick Steves books and DVDs are available at bookstores and through online booksellers.
Rick Steves guidebooks are published by Avalon Travel, a member of the Perseus Books Group.
Rick Steves apps are produced by Übermind, a boutique Seattle-based software consultancy firm.

Avalon Travel
a member of the Perseus Books Group
1700 Fourth Street
Berkeley, CA 94710

Text © 2009 by Rick Steves.
Maps © 2009 by Europe Through the Back Door.
Printed in the United States of America by Worzalla.
First printing November 2009.

ISBN 978-1-59880-494-2

For the latest on Rick's lectures, guidebooks, tours, public radio show, and public television
series, contact Europe Through the Back Door, Box 2009, Edmonds, WA 98020, tel.
425/771-8303, fax 425/771-0833, www.ricksteves.com, rick@ricksteves.com.

Europe Through the Back Door Senior Editor: Jennifer Madison Davis
ETBD Editors: Gretchen Strauch, Cathy McDonald, Tom Griffin, Cathy Lu, Sarah
    McCormic
ETBD Managing Editor: Risa Laib
Avalon Travel Senior Editor and Series Manager: Madhu Prasher
Avalon Travel Project Editor: Kelly Lydick
Copy Editor: Judith Brown
Proofreader: Naomi Adler-Dancis
Production & Typesetting: McGuire Barber Design
Cover Design: Kimberly Glyder Design
Graphic Content Director: Laura VanDeventer
Maps & Graphics: David C. Hoerlein, Brice Ticen, Laura VanDeventer, Lauren Mills,
    Barb Geisler, Mike Morgenfeld
Front Matter Color Photos: p. i and p. viii, © Pat O'Connor
Cover Photo: Giant's Causeway © Pat O'Connor
Photography: Pat O'Connor, Rick Steves, David C. Hoerlein

ABOUT THE AUTHORS

RICK STEVES

Rick Steves is on a mission: to help make European travel accessible and meaningful for Americans. Rick has spent four months every year since 1973 exploring Europe. He's researched and written more than 30 travel guidebooks, writes and hosts the public television series *Rick Steves' Europe*, and also produces and hosts the weekly public radio show *Travel with Rick Steves.* With the help of his hardworking staff of 70 at Europe Through the Back Door, Rick organizes tours of Europe and offers an information-packed website (www.ricksteves.com). Rick, his wife (and favorite travel partner) Anne, and their two teenage children, Andy and Jackie, call Edmonds, just north of Seattle, home.

PAT O'CONNOR

Irish-American Pat O'Connor first journeyed to Ireland in 1981, and was hooked by the history and passion of the feisty Irish culture. Frequent return visits led to his partnership with Rick Steves and his work as a tour guide and co-author of this book. Pat loves all things Hibernian (except the black pudding) and thrives on the adventures that occur as he annually slogs the bogs in search of new Irish travel discoveries. When he's not in Europe, Pat lives in Edmonds, splitting his time between helping travelers who visit Rick's Travel Center, and fine-tuning photos and maps for the guidebook series.